THE

SACONTALA

THE SACONTALA OR THE FATAL RING.

KALIDASA

TRANSLATED BY

SIR WILLIAM JONES., KNIGH

GYAN

Published by

Gyan Publishing House
5, Ansari Road
Daryaganj, New Delhi-110002
Phone: 011-47034999, 9811692060
E-mail: books@gyanbooks.com

Distribution Network
gyanbooks.com
India, USA, Canada, UK, Australia, France

ISBN : 978-81-212-9436-2 (PB)
First Published, 1875

2nd Impression 2023

Printed at: Gyan Press, Delhi.

THE SACONTALA
Translator : SIR WILLAM JONES

THE SACONTALA:

OR

THE FATAL RING.

TRANSLATED BY

SIR WILLIAM JONES., KNIGH

ONE OF THE JUDGES OF HER MAJESTY'S LATE SUPREME COURT, FORT WILLIAM, BENGAL, FOUNDER AND FIRST PRESIDENT OF THE ASIATIC SOCIETY OF BENGAL.

REPUBLISHED BY

JOGENDRA NATH GHOSE.

CALCUTTA:

TRÜBNER & CO., 57 & 59, LUDGATE HILL, LONDON.

1875.

TO

HIS HIGHNESS THE MAHARAJA OF

VIJOYNAGRAM G. C. S. I.

THIS NOBLE TRANSLATION

OF

SACONTALA

OF

KALIDASA

BY

SIR WILLIAM JONES., KT.

IS DEDICATED

IN ADMIRATION OF

HIS HIGHNES'S RENOWNED PHILANTHROPY

AND

GREAT TALENTS

BY THE HUMBLE SERVANT

The Publisher.

PREFACE.

IN one of the letters which bear the title of EDIFYING, though most of them swarm with ridiculous errors, and all must be consulted with extreme diffidence, I met, some years ago, with the following passage: "In the north of India there are many books, called Nátac, which, as the Bráhmens assert, contain a large portion of ancient history without any mixture of fable;" and having an eager desire to know the real state of this empire before the conquest of it by the Savages of the North, I was very solicitous, on my arrival in Bengal, to procure access to those books, either by the help of translations, if they had been translated, or by learning the language in which they were originally composed, and which I had yet a stronger inducement to learn from its connection with the administration of justice to the Hindûs; but when I was able to converse with the Bráhmens, they assured me that the Nátacs were not histories, and abounded with fables; that they were extremely popular works, and consisted of conversations in prose and verse, held before ancient Rájás in their public assemblies, on an infinite variety of subjects, and in various dialects of India: this definition gave me no very distinct idea; but I concluded that they were dialogues on moral or literary topics; whilst other Europeans, whom I consulted, had understood from the natives that they were discourses on dancing, music, or poetry. At length a very sensible Bráhmen, named Rádhácánt, who had long been attentive to English manners, removed all my doubts, and gave me no less delight than surprise, by telling me that our nation had compositions of the same sort, which were publicly represented at Calcutta in the cold season, and bore the name, as he had been informed, of plays. Resolving at my leisure to read the best of them, I asked which of their Nátacs was most universally esteemed; and he answered without hesitation, Sacontalá, supporting his opinion, as usual among the Pandits, by a couplet to this effect: "The ring of Sacontalá, in which the fourth act, and four stanzas of that act, are eminently brilliant, displays all the rich exuberance of Cálidása's genius." I soon procured a correct copy of it; and, assisted by my teacher Rámalóchan, began with translating it verbally into Latin, which bears so great a resemblance to Sanscrit, that it is more convenient than any modern language for a scrupulous interlineary version: I then turned it word for word into English, and afterwards, without adding or suppressing any material sentence, disengaged it from the stiffness of a foreign idiom, and prepared the faithful translation of the Indian drama, which I now present to the Public as a most pleasing and authentic picture of old Hindû manners, and one of the greatest curiosities that the literature of Asia has yet brought to light.

Dramatic poetry must have been immemorially ancient in the Indian empire: the invention of it is commonly ascribed to Bheret, a sage believed to have been inspired, who invented also a system of music which bears his name; but this opinion of its origin is rendered very doubtful by the universal belief, that the first Sanscrit verse ever heard by mortals was pronounced in a burst of resentment by the great Válmic, who flourished in the silver age of the world, and was author of an Epic Poem on the war of his contemporary, Ráma, king of Ayódhyà; so that no drama in verse could have been represented before his time; and the Indians have a wild story, that the first regular play, on the same subject with the Rámáyan, was composed by Hanumat or Pávan, who commanded an army of Satyrs or Mountaineers in Ráma's expedition against Lancá: they add that he engraved it on a smooth rock, which, being dissatisfied with his composition, he hurled into the sea; and that, many years after, a learned prince ordered expert divers to take impressions of the poem on wax, by which means the drama was in great measure restored; and my Pandit assures me that he is in possession of it. By whomsoever or in whatever age this species of entertainment was invented, it is very certain, that it was carried to great perfection in its kind, when Vicramáditya, who reigned in the first century before Christ, gave encouragement to poets, philologers, and mathematicians, at a time when the Britons were as unlettered and unpolished as the army of Hanumat: nine men of genius, commonly called the nine gems, attended his court, and were splendidly supported by his bounty; and Cálidás is unanimously allowed to have been the brightest of them.—A modern epigram was lately repeated to me, which does so much honor to the author of Sacontalá, that I cannot forbear exhibiting a literal version of it: "Poetry was the sportful daughter of Válmic, and, having been educated by Vyása, she chose Cálidás for her bridegroom after the manner of Viderbha: she was the mother of Amara, Sundar, Sanc'ha, Dhanic; but now, old and decrepit, her beauty faded, and her unadorned feet slipping as she walks, in whose cottage does she disdain to take shelter?"

All the other works of our illustrious poet, the Shakespeare of India, that have yet come to my knowledge, are a second play, in five acts, entitled Urvasí; an heroic poem, or rather a series of poems in one book, on the Children of the Sun; another, with perfect unity of action, on the Birth of Cumára, god of war; two or three love tales in verse; and an excellent little work on Sanscrit Metre, precisely in the manner of Terentianus; but he is believed by some to have revised the works of Válmic and Vyása, and to have corrected the perfect editions of them which are now current; this at least is admitted by all, that he stands next in reputation to those venerable bards; and we must regret, that he has left only two dramatic poems, especially as the stories in his Raghuvansa would have supplied him with a number of excellent subjects.—Some of his contemporaries, and other Hindû poets even to our own times, have composed so many tragedies, comedies, farces, and musical pieces, that the Indian theatre would fill as many volumes as that of any nation in ancient or modern Europe; all the Pandits assert that their plays are innumerable; and, on my first inquiries concerning them, I had notice of more than thirty, which they consider as the flower of their Nátacs, among which the Malignant Child, the Rape of Ushá, the Taming of Durvásas, the Seizure of the Lock, Málati and Mádhava with five or six dramas on the adventures of their incarnate gods, are the most admired after those of Cálidás. They are all in verse, where the dialogue is elevated; and in prose where it is familiar; the men of rank and learning are represented speaking pure Sanscrit, and the women Prácrit, which is little more than the language of the Bráhmens melted down by a delicate articulation to the softness of Italian; while the low persons of the drama speak the vulgar dialects of the several provinces which they are supposed to inhabit.

The play of Sacontalá must have been very popular when it was first represented; for the Indian empire was then in full vigour, and the national vanity must have been highly flattered by the magnificent introduction of those kings and heroes in whom the Hindûs gloried; the scenery must have been splendid and beautiful; and there is good reason to believe, that the court at Avanti was equal in brilliancy during the reign of Vicramáditya, to that of any monarch in any age or country.—Dushmanta, the hero of the piece, appears in the chronological tables of the Bráhmens among the Children of the Moon, and in the twenty-first generation after the flood; so that, if we can at all rely on the chronology of the Hindûs, he was nearly contemporary with Obed, or Jesse; and Puru, his most celebrated ancestor, was the fifth in descent from Budha, or Mercury, who married, they say, a daughter of the pious king whom Vishnu preserved in an ark from the universal deluge: his eldest son Bheret was the illustrious progenitor of Curu, from whom Pàndu was lineally descended, and in whose family the Indian Apollo became incarnate; whence the poem, next in fame to the Rámáyan, is called Mahábhárat.

As to the machinery of the drama, it is taken from the system of mythology, which prevails to this day, and which it would require a large volume to explain; but we cannot help remarking that the deities introduced in the Fatal Ring are clearly allegorical personages. Maríchi, the first production of Brahmà, or the Creative Power, signifies light, that subtil fluid which was created before its reservoir, the sun, as water was created before the sea Casyapa, the offspring of Maríchi, seems to be a personification of infinite space, comprehending innumerable worlds; and his children by Aditi, or his active power (unless Aditi mean the primeval day, and Diti, his other wife, the night), are Indra, or the visible firmament, and the twelve Adityas, or suns, presiding over as many months.

On the characters and conduct of the play I shall offer no criticism; because I am convinced that the tastes of men differ as much as their sentiments and passions, and that, in feeling the beauties of art, as in smelling flowers, tasting fruits, viewing prospects, and hearing melody, every individual must be guided by his own sensations and the incommunicable associations of his own ideas. This only I may add, that if Sacontalá should ever be acted in India, where alone it could be acted with perfect knowledge of Indian dresses, manners, and scenery, the piece might easily be reduced to five acts of a moderate length, by throwing the third act into the second, and the sixth into the fifth; for it must be confessed that the whole of Dushmanta's conversation with his buffoon, and great part of his courtship in the hermitage might be omitted without any injury to the drama.

It is my anxious wish that others may take the pains to learn Sanscrit, and may be persuaded to translate the works of Cálidás: I shall hardly again employ my leisure in a task so foreign to my professional (which are, in truth, my favorite) studies; and have no intention of translating any other book from any language, except the Law Tract of Menu, and the new Digest of Indian and Arabian laws; but, to show, that the Bráhmens, at least, do not think polite literature incompatible with jurisprudence, I cannot avoid mentioning, that the venerable compiler of the Hindû Digest, who is now in the eighty-sixth year, has the whole play of Sacontalá by heart, as he proved when I last conversed with him, to my entire conviction. Lest, however, I should hereafter seem to have changed a resolution which I mean to keep inviolate, I think it proper to say, that I have already translated four or five other books, and among them the Hitópadésa, which I undertook, merely as an exercise in learning Sanscrit, three years before I knew that Mr. Wilkins, without whose aid I should never have learnt it, had any thought of giving the same work to the public.

PERSONS OF THE DRAMA.

Dushmanta, Emperor of India.

Sacontalá, the Heroine of the Piece.

Anusûyá, *Priyamvadá*, Damsels attendant on her.

Mádhavyá, the Emperor's Buffoon.

Gautamì, an old female Hermit.

Sárngarava, *Sáradwata*, two Bràhmens.

Canna, Foster-father of Sacontalá.

Cumbhìlaca, a Fisherman.

Misracésí, a Nymph.

Mátali, Charioteer of Indra.

A little Boy.

Casyapa, *Aditi*, Deities, Parents of Indra.

Officers of State and Police, Bràhmens, Damsels, Hermits, Pupils, Chamberlas, Warders of the Palace, Messengers, and Attendants.

THE PROLOGUE.

A Bráhmen *pronounces the benediction.*

WATER was the first work of the Creator; and Fire receives the oblations ordained by law; the Sacrifice is performed with solemnity; the Two Lights of heaven distinguish time; the subtil Ether, which is the vehicle of sound, pervades the universe; the Earth is the natural parent of all increase; and by Air all things breathing are animated: may I'SA, the God of Nature, apparent in these eight forms, bless and sustain you!

The Manager *enters.*

Man. What occasion is there for a long speech?—[*Looking towards the dressing room*]—When your decorations, Madam, are completed, be pleased to come forward.

An Actress *enters.*

Actr. I attend, Sir.—What are your commands?

Man. This, Madam, is the numerous and polite assembly of the famed Hero, our king Vicramáditya, the patron of every delightful art; and before this audience we must do justice to a new production of Cálidás, a dramatic piece, entitled Sacontalá, or, The Fatal Ring: it is requested, therefore, that all will be attentive.

Actr. Who, Sir, could be inattentive to an entertainment so well intended?

Man. [*Smiling*] I will speak, Madam, without reserve.—As far as an enlightened audience receive pleasure from our theatrical talents, and express it, so far, and no farther, I set a value on them; but my own mind is diffident of its powers, how strongly soever exerted.

Actr. You judge rightly in measuring your own merit by the degree of pleasure which this assembly may receive; but its value, I trust, will presently appear.—Have you any farther commands?

Man. What better can you do, since you are now on the stage, than exhilarate the souls, and gratify the sense, of our auditory with a song?

Actr. Shall I sing the description of a season? and which of the seasons do you choose to hear described?

Man. No finer season could be selected than the summer, which is actually begun, and abounds with delights. How sweet is the close of a summer day, which invites our youth to bathe in pure streams, and induces gentle slumber under the shades refreshed by sylvan breezes, which have passed over the blooming Pátalis and stolen their fragrance!

Actr. [*Singing*] "Mark how the soft blossoms of the Nágacésar are lightly kissed by the bees! Mark how the damsels delicately place behind their ears the flowers of Sirísha!"

Man. A charming strain! the whole company sparkles, as it were, with admiration; and the musical mode to which the words are adapted, has filled their souls with rapture. By what other performance can we ensure a continuance of their favor?

Actr. Oh! by none better than by the Fatal Ring, which you have just announced.

Man. How could I forget it! In that moment I was lulled to distraction by the melody of thy voice, which allured my heart, as the king Dushmanta is now allured by the swift antelope.

[*They both go out.*

SACONTALÁ;

OR,

THE FATAL RING.

ACT I.

SCENE—A FOREST.

DUSHMANTA, *in a car, pursuing an antelope, with a bow and quiver, attended by his* Charioteer.

Char. [*Looking at the antelope, and then at the king.*]

WHEN I cast my eye on that black antelope, and on thee, O king, with thy braced bow, I see before me, as it were, the God Mahésa chasing a hart, with his bow, named pináca, braced in his left hand.

Dushm. The fleet animal has given us a long chase. Oh! there he runs, with his neck bent gracefully, looking back, from time to time, at the car which follows him. Now, through fear of a descending shaft, he contracts his forehand, and extends his flexible haunches; and now, through fatigue, he pauses to nibble the grass in his path with his mouth half opened. See how he springs and bounds with long steps, lightly skimming the ground, and rising high in the air! And now so rapid in his flight, that he is scarce discernible!

Char. The ground was uneven, and the horses were checked in their course. He has taken advantage of our delay. It is level now, and we may easily overtake him.

Dushm. Loosen the reins.

Char. As the king commands.—[*He drives the car first at full speed, and then gently.*]—He could not escape. The horses were not even touched by the clouds of dust which they raised; they tossed their manes, erected their ears, and rather glided than galloped over the smooth plain.

Dushm. They soon outran the swift antelope.—Objects which, from their distance, appeared minute, presently became larger: what was really divided, seemed united, as we passed; and what was in truth bent, seemed straight. So swift was the motion of the wheels, that nothing, for many moments, was either distant or near. [*He fixes an arrow in his bowstring.*

[*Behind the scenes.*] He must not be slain. This antelope, O king, has an asylum in our forest: he must not be slain.

Char. [*Listening and looking.*] Just as the animal presents a fair mark for your arrow, two hermits are advancing to interrupt your aim.

Dushm. Then stop the car.

Char. The king is obeyed. [*He draws in the reins.*

Enter a HERMIT *and his* PUPIL.

Herm. [*Raising his hands.*] Slay not, O mighty sovereign, slay not a poor fawn, who has found a place of refuge. No, surely, no; he must not be hurt. An arrow in the delicate body of a deer would be like fire in a bale of cotton. Compared with thy keen shafts, how weak must be the tender hide of a young antelope! Replace quickly, oh! replace the arrow which thou hast aimed. The weapons of you kings and warriors are destined for the relief of the oppressed, not for the destruction of the guiltless.

Dushm. [*Saluting them.*] It is replaced.

[*He placed the arrow in his quiver.*

Herm. [*With joy.*] Worthy is that act of thee, most illustrious of monarchs; worthy, indeed, of a prince descended from Puru. Mayst thou have a son adorned with virtues, a sovereign of the world!

Pup. [*Elevating both his hands.*] Oh! by all means, may thy son be adorned with every virtue, a sovereign of the world!

Dushm. [*Bowing to them.*] My head bears with reverence the order of a Bràhmen.

Herm. Great King, we came hither to collect wood for a solemn sacrifice; and this forest, on the banks of the Malinì, affords an asylum to the wild animals protected by Sacontalá, whom our holy preceptor Canna has received as a sacred deposit. If you have no other avocation, enter yon grove, and let the rights of hospitality be duly performed. Having seen with your own eyes the virtuous behaviour of those whose only wealth is their piety, but whose worldly cares are now at an end, you will then exclaim, "How many good subjects are defended by this arm, which the bowstring has made callous!"

Dushm. Is the master of your family at home?

Herm. Our preceptor is gone to Sómatírt'ha, in hopes of deprecating some calamity, with which destiny threatens the irreproachable Sacontalà; and he has charged her, in his absence, to receive all guests with due honor.

Dushm. Holy man, I will attend her; and she, having observed my devotion, will report it favourably to the venerable sage.

Both. Be it so; and we depart on our own business.

[*The* Hermit *and his* Pupil *go out.*

Dushm. Drive on the car. By visiting the abode of holiness, we shall purify our souls.

Char. As the king (may his life be long!) commands. [*He drives on.*

Dushm. [*Looking on all sides.*] That we are near the dwelling-place of pious hermits, would clearly have appeared, even if it had not been told.

Char. By what marks?

Dushm. Do you not observe them? See under yon trees the hallowed grains which have been scattered on the ground, while the tender female parrots were feeding their unfledged young in their pendent nests. Mark in other places the shining pieces of polishd stone which have bruised the oily fruit of the sacred Ingudì. Look at the young fawns, which, having acquired confidence in man, and accustomed themselves to the sound of his voice, frisk at pleasure, without varying their course. Even the surface of the river is reddened with lines of consecrated bark, which float down its stream. Look again ; the roots of yon trees are bathed in the waters of holy pools, which quiver as the breeze plays upon them ; and the glowing lustre of yon fresh leaves is obscured, for a time, by smoke that rises from oblations of clarified butter. See too, where the young roes graze, without apprehension from our approach, on the lawn before yonder garden, were the tops of the sacrificial grass, cut for some religious rite, are sprinkled around.

Char. I now observe all those marks of some holy habitation.

Dushm. [*Turning aside.*] This awful sanctuary, my friend, must not be violated. Here, therefore, stop the car ; that I may descend.

Char. I hold in the reins. The king may descend at his pleasure.

Dushm. [*Having descended, and looking at his own dress.*] Groves devoted to religion must be entered in humbler habiliments. Take these regal ornaments ;—[*the* Charioteer *receives them*]—and, whilst I am observing those who inhabit this retreat, let the horses be watered and dressed.

Char. Be it as you direct ! [*He goes out.*

Dushm. [*Walking round and looking.*] Now then I enter the sanctuary.—[*He enters the grove.*]—Oh ! this place must be holy my right arm throbs.—[*Pausing and considering.*]—What new acquisition does this omen promise in a sequestered grove ? But the gates of predestined events are in all places open.

[*Behind the scenes.*] Come hither, my beloved companions ; Oh ! come hither.

Dushm. [*Listening.*] Hah ! I hear female voices to the right of yon arbour. I am resolved to know who are conversing.—[*He walks round and looks.*]—There are some damsels, I see, belonging to the hermit's family who carry water-pots of different sizes proportioned to their strength, and are going to water the delicate plants. Oh! how charmingly they look! If the beauty of maids who dwell in woodland retreats cannot easily be found in the recesses of a palace, the garden flowers must make room for the blossoms of the forest, which excel them in colour and fragrance. [*He stands gazing at them.*

Enter Sacontalá, Anusúyá, *and* Priyamvadá.

Anu. O my Sacontalá, it is in thy society that the trees of our father Canna seem to me delightful: it well becomes thee, who art soft as the freshblown Mallicá, to fill with water the canals which have been dug round these tender shrubs.

Sac. It is not only in obedience to our father that I thus employ myself, though that were a sufficient motive, but I really feel the affection of a sister for these young plants.

[*Watering them.*

Pri. My beloved friend, the shrubs which you have watered flower in the summer, which is now begun: let us give water to those which have passed their flowering time; for our virtue will be the greater when it is wholly disinterested.

Sac. Excellent advice! [*Watering other plants.*

Dushm. [*Aside in transport.*] How! is that Canna's daughter, Sacontalá?—[*With surprise.*]—The venerable sage must have an unfeeling heart, since he has allotted a mean employment to so lovely a girl, and has dressed her in a coarse mantle of woven bark. He, who could wish that so beautiful a creature, who at first sight ravishes my soul should endure the hardships of his austere devotion, would attempt, I suppose, to cleave the hard wood Samì with a leaf of the blue lotos. Let me retire behind this tree, that I may gaze on her charms without diminishing her confidence. [*He retires.*

Sac. My friend Priyamvadá has tied this mantle of bark so closely over my bosom that it gives me pain: Anusúyá, I request you to untie it. [Anusúyá *unties the mantle.*

Pri. [*Laughing.*] Well, my sweet friend, enjoy, while you may, that youthful prime which gives your bosom so beautiful a swell.

Dushm. [*Aside.*] Admirably spoken, Priyamvadá ! No ; her charms cannot be hidden, even though a robe of intertwisted fibres be thrown over her shoulders, and conceal a part of her bosom, like a veil of yellow leaves enfolding a radiant flower. The water lily, though dark moss may settle on its head, is nevertheless beautiful ; and the moon with dewy beams is rendered yet brighter by its black spots. The bark itself acquires elegance from the features of a girl with antelope's eyes, and rather augments than diminishes my ardour. Many are the rough stalks which support the water lily ; but many and exquisite are the blossoms which hang on them.

Sac. [*Looking before her.*] Yon Amra tree, my friends, points with the finger of its leaves, which the gale gently agitates, and seems inclined to whisper some secret. I will go near it.

[*They all approach the tree.*

Pri. O my Sacontalá, let us remain some time in this shade.

Sac. Why here particularly ?

Pri. Because the Amra tree seems wedded to you, who are graceful as the blooming creeper which twines round it.

Sac. Properly are you named Priyamvadá, or speaking kindly.

Dushm. [*Aside.*] She speaks truly. Yes ; her lip glows like the tender leaflet ; her arms resemble two flexible stalks ; and youthful beauty shines, like a blossom, in all her lineaments.

Anu. See, my Sacontalá, how yon fresh Mallicà, which you have surnamed Vanàdósinì, or Delight of the Grove, has chosen the sweet Amra for her bridegroom.

Sac. [*Approaching, and looking at it with pleasure.*] How charming is the season, when the nuptials even of plants are thus publicly celebrated ! [*She stands admiring it.*

Pri. [*Smiling.*] Do you know, my Anusúyá, why Sacontalá gazes on the plants with such rapture ?

Anu. No, indeed : I was trying to guess. Pray, tell me.

Pri. "As the Grove's Delight is united to a suitable tree, thus I too hope for a bridegroom to my mind."—That is her private thought at this moment.

Sac. Such are the flights of your own imagination.

[*Inverting the water-pot.*

Anu. Here is a plant, Sacontalá, which you have forgotten, though it has grown up, like yourself, under the fostering care of our father Canna.

Sac. Then I shall forget myself.—O wonderful !—[*approaching the plant.*]—O Priyamvadá ! [*looking at it with joy*] I have delightful tidings for you.

Pri. What tidings, my beloved, for me ?

Sac. This Mádhavi-creeper, though it be not the usual time for flowering, is covered with gay blossoms from its root to its top.

Both. [*Approaching it hastily.*] Is it really so, sweet friend ?

Sac Is it so ? look yourselves.

Pri. [*With eagerness.*] From this omen, Sacontalá, I announce you an excellent husband, who will very soon take you by the hand. [*Both girls look at* Sacontalá.

Sac. [*Displeased.*] A strange fancy of yours !

Pri. Indeed, my beloved, I speak not jestingly. I heard something from our father Canna. Your nurture of these plants has prospered; and thence it is, that I foretel your approaching nuptials.

Anu. It is thence, my Priyamvadá, that she has watered them with so much alacrity.

Sac. The Mádhavi plant is my sister: can I do otherwise than cherish her ? [*Pouring water on it.*

Dushm. [*Aside.*] I fear she is of the same religious order with her foster-father. Or has a mistaken apprehension risen in my mind ? My warm heart is so attached to her, that she cannot but be a fit match for a man of the military class. The doubt which awhile perplex the good, are soon removed by the prevalence of their strong inclinations. I am enamoured of her; and she cannot, therefore, be the daughter of a Bráhmen, whom I could not marry.

Sac. [*Moving her head.*] Alas ! a bee has left the blossom of this Mallicá, and is fluttering round my face.

[*She expresses uneasiness.*

Dushm. [*Aside, with affection.*] How often have I seen our court damsels affectedly turn their heads aside from some roving insect, merely to display their graces! but this rural charmer knits her brows, and gracefully moves her eyes through fear only, without art or affectation. Oh! happy bee, who touchest the corner of that eye beautifully trembling; who, approaching the tip of that ear, murmurest as softly as if thou wert whispering a secret of love; and who sippest nectar, while she waves her graceful hand, from that lip, which contains all the treasures of delight! Whilst I am solicitous to know in what family she was born, thou art enjoying bliss, which to me would be supreme felicity.

Sac. Disengage me, I entreat, from this importunate insect, which quite baffles my efforts.

Pri. What power have we to deliver you? The king Dushmanta is the sole defender of our consecrated groves.

Dushm. [*Aside.*] This is a good occasion for me to discover myself—[*advancing a little.*]—I must not, I will not, fear. Yet—[*checking himself and retiring*]—my royal character will thus abruptly be known to them. No; I will appear as a simple stranger, and claim the duties of hospitality.

Sac. This impudent bee will not rest. I will remove to another place. [*Stepping aside and looking round.*]—Away! away! He follows me wherever I go. Deliver me, oh! deliver me from this distress.

Dushm. [*Advancing hastily.*] Ah! While the race of Puru govern the world, and restrain even the most profligate, by good laws well administered, has any man the audacity to molest the lovely daughters of pious hermits?

[*They look at him with emotion.*

Anu. Sir, no man is here audacious; but this damsel, our beloved friend, was teased by a fluttering bee.

[*Both girl look at* Socontalá.

Dushm. [*Approaching her.*] Damsel, may thy devotion prosper!

Sacontalá *looks on the ground, bashful and silent.*

Anu. Our guest must be received with due honors.

Pri. Stranger, you are welcome. Go, my Sacontalá; bring from the cottage a basket of fruit and flowers. This river will, in the mean time, supply water for his feet.

[*Looking at the water-pots.*

Dushm. Holy maid, the gentleness of thy speech does me sufficient honor.

Anu. Sit down awhile on this bank of earth, spread with the leaves of Septaperna: the shade is refreshing, and our lord must want repose after his journey.

Dushm. You too must all be fatigued by your hospitable attentions: rest yourselves, therefore, with me.

Pri. [*Aside to* Sacontalá.] Come, let us all be seated: our guest is contented with our reception of him.

[*They all seat themselves.*

Sac. [*Aside.*] At the sight of this youth I feel an emotion scarce consistent with a grove devoted to piety.

Dushm. [*Gazing at them alternately.*] How well your friendship agrees, holy damsels, with the charming equality of your ages and of your beauties!

Pri. [*Aside to* Anusúyá.] Who can this be, my Anusúyá? The union of delicacy with robustness in his form, and of sweetness with dignity in his discourse, indicate a character fit for ample dominion.

Anu. [*Aside to* Priyamvadá.] I too have been admiring him. I must ask him a few questions.—[*Aloud.*] Your sweet speech, Sir, gives me confidence. What imperial family is embellished by our noble guest? What is his native country? Surely it must be afflicted by his absence from it. What, I pray, could induce you to humiliate that exalted form of yours by visiting a forest peopled only by simple anchorites?

Sac. [*Aside.*] Perplex not thyself, oh my heart! let the faithful Anusúyá direct with her counsel the thoughts which rise in thee.

Dushm. [*Aside.*] How shall I reveal, or how shall I disguise myself?—[*Musing.*]—Be it so.—[*Aloud to* Anusúyá.] Excellent lady, I am a student of the Véda, dwelling in the city of our king, descended from Puru; and being occupied in the discharge of religious and moral duties, am come hither to behold the sanctuary of virtue.

Anu. Holy men, employed like you, are our lords and masters.

[Sacontalá *looks modest, yet with affection; while her companions gaze alternately at her and at the king.*

Anu. [*Aside to* Sacontalá.] Oh! if our venerable father were present—

Sac. What if he were?

Anu. He would entertain our guest with a variety of refreshments.

Sac. [*Pretending displeasure.*] Go too; you had some other idea in your head; I will not listen to you. [*She sits apart.*

Dushm. [*Aside to* Anusúyá and Priyamvadá.] In my turn holy damsels, allow me to ask one question concerning your lovely friend.

Both. The request, Sir, does us honour.

Dushm. The sage Canna, I know, is ever intent upon the great Being; and must have declined all earthly connections. How then can this damsel be, as it is said, his daughter?

Anu. Let our lord hear. There is, in the family of Cusa, a pious prince of extensive power, eminent in devotion and in arms.

Dushm. You speak, no doubt, of Causica, the sage and monarch.

Anu. Know, Sir, that he is in truth her father; while Canna bears that reverend name, because he brought her up, since she was left an infant.

Dushm. Left? the word excites my curiosity; and raises in me a desire of knowing her whole story.

Anu. You shall hear it, Sir, in few words.—When that sage king had begun to gather the fruits of his austere devotion, the gods of Swerga became apprehensive of his increasing power, and sent the nymph Ménacá to frustrate, by her allurements, the full effect of his piety.

Dushm. Is a mortal's piety so tremendous to the inferior deities? What was the event?

Anu. In the bloom of the vernal season, Causica, beholding the beauty of the celestial nymph, and wasted by the gale of desire— [*She stops and looks modest.*

Dushm. I now see the whole. Sacontalá then is the daughter of a king, by a nymph of the lower heaven.

Anu. Even so.

Dushm. [*Aside.*] The desire of my heart is gratified.—[*Aloud.*] How, indeed, could her transcendent beauty be the portion of mortal birth? Yon light, that sparkles with tremulous beams, proceeds not from a terrestrial cavern. [Sacontalá *sits modestly, with her eyes on the ground.*

Dushm. [*Again aside.*] Happy man that I am! Now has my fancy an ample range. Yet, having heard the pleasantry of her companions on the subject of her nuptials, I am divided with anxious doubt, whether she be not wholly destined for a religious life.

Pri. [*Smiling, and looking first at* Sacontalá, *then at the king.*] Our lord seems desirous of asking other questions.

[Sacontalá *rebukes* Priyamvadá *with her hand.*

Dushm. You know my very heart. I am, indeed, eager to learn the whole of this charmer's life; and must put one question more.

Pri. Why should you muse on it so long?—[*Aside.*] One would think this religious man was forbidden by his vows to court a pretty woman.

Dushm. This I ask. Is the strict rule of a hermit so far to be observed by Canna, that he cannot dispose of his daughter in mariage, but must check the natural impulse of juvenile love? Can she (oh preposterous fate!) be destined to reside for life among her favourite antelopes, the black lustre of whose eyes is far surpassed by hers?

Pri. Hitherto, Sir, our friend has lived happy in this consecrated forest, the abode of her spiritual father; but it is now his intention to unite her with a bridegroom equal to herself.

Dushm. [*Aside, with ecstasy.*] Exult, oh my heart, exult. All doubt is removed; and what before thou wouldst have dreaded as a flame, may now be approached as a gem inestimable.

Sac. [*Seeming angry.*] Anusúyá, I will stay here no longer.

Anu. Why so I pray ?

Sac. I will go to the holy matron Gautamí, and let her know how impertinently our Priyamvadá has been prattling. [*She rises.*

Anu. It will not be decent, my love, for an inhabitant of this hallowed wood to retire before a guest has received complete honor. [Sacontalá, *giving no answer*, *offers to go.*

Dushm. [*Aside.*] Is she then departing ?—[*He rises, as if going to stop her, but checks himself.*]—The actions of a passionate lover are as precipitate as his mind is agitated. Thus I, whose passion impelled me to follow the hermit's daughter, am restrained by a sense of duty.

Pri. [*Going up to* Sacontalá.] My angry friend, you must not retire.

Sac. [*Stepping back and frowning.*] What should detain me ?

Pri. You owe me the labour, according to our agreement, of watering two more shrubs. Pay me first, to acquit your conscience, and then depart, if you please. [*Holding her.*

Dushm. The damsel is fatigued, I imagine, by pouring so much water on the cherished plants. Her arms, graced with palms like fresh blossoms, hang carelessly down; her bosom heaves with strong breathing; and now her dishevelled locks, from which the string has dropped, are held by one of her lovely hands. Suffer me, therefore, thus to discharge the debt.—[*Giving his ring to* Priyamvadà. *Both damsels, reading the name* Dushmanta, *inscribed on the ring, look with surprise at each other.*]—It is a toy unworthy of your fixed attention ; but I value it as gift from the king.

Pri. Then you ought not, Sir, to part with it. Her debt is from this moment discharged on your word only. [*She returns the ring.*

Anu. You are now released, Sacontalá, by this benevolent lord—or favored, perhaps, by a monarch himself. To what place will you now retire ?

Sac. [*Aside.*] Must I not wonder at all this if I preserve my senses?

Pri. Are not you going, Sacontalá?

Sac. Am I your subject? I shall go when it pleases me.

Dushm. [*Aside looking at* Sacontalá.] Either she is affected towards me, as I am towards her, or I am distracted with joy. She mingles not her discourse with mine; yet, when I speak, she listens attentively. She commands not her actions in my presence; and her eyes are engaged on me alone.

Behind the scenes.] Oh pious hermits, preserve the animals of this hallowed forest! The King Dushmanta is hunting in it. The dust raised by the hoofs of his horses, which pound the pebbles ruddy as early dawn, falls like a swarm of blighting insects on the consecrated boughs which sustain your mantles of woven bark, moist with the water of the stream in which you have bathed.

Dushm. [*Aside.*] Alas! my officers, who are searching for me, have indiscreetly disturbed this holy retreat.

Again behind the scenes.] Beware, ye hermits, of yon elephant, who comes overturning all that oppose him; now he fixes his trunk with violence on a lofty branch that obstructs his way; and now he is entangled in the twining stalks of the Vratati. How are our sacred rites interrupted! How are the protected herds dispersed! The wild elephant, alarmed at the new appearance of a car, lays our forest waste.

Dushm. [*Aside.*] How unwillingly am I offending the devout foresters! Yes; I must go to them instantly.

Pri. Noble stranger, we are confounded with dread of the enraged elephant. With your permission, therefore, we retire to the hermit's cottage.

Anu. O Sacontalá, the venerable matron will be much distressed on your account. Come quickly, that we may be all safe together.

Sac. [*Walking slowly.*] I am stopped, alas! by a sudden pain in my side.

Dushm. Be not alarmed, amiable damsels. It shall be my care that no disturbance happen in your sacred groves.

Pri. Excellent stranger, we were wholly unacquainted with your station; and you will forgive us, we hope, for the offence of intermitting awhile the honors due to you: but we humbly request that you will give us once more the pleasure of seeing you, though you have not now been received with perfect hospitality.

Dushm. You depreciate your merits. The sight of you, sweet damsels, has sufficiently honored me.

Sac. My foot, O Anusúyá, is hurt by this pointed blade of Cusa grass; and now my loose vest of bark is caught by a branch of the Curuvaca. Help me to disentangle myself, and support me.—[*She goes out, looking from time to time at* Dushmanta, *and supported by the damsels.*]

Dushm. [*Sighing.*] They are all departed; and I too, alas! must depart. For how short a moment have I been blessed with a sight of the incomparable Sacontalá! I will send my attendants to the city, and take my station at no great distance from this forest. I cannot, in truth, divert my mind from the sweet occupation of gazing on her. How, indeed, should I otherwise occupy it? My body moves onward; but my restless heart runs back to her; like a light flag borne on a staff against the wind, and fluttering in an opposite direction. [*He goes out.*]

ACT II.

SCENE—*A* PLAIN, *with royal pavilions on the skirt of the forest.*
Mádhavya. [*Sighing and lamenting.*]

STRANGE recreation this?—Ah me! I am wearied to death.—My royal friend has an unaccountable taste.—What can I think of a king so passionately fond of chasing unprofitable quadrupeds?—"Here runs an antelope!—there goes a boar!"—Such is our only conversation.—Even at noon, in excessive heat, when not a tree in the forest has a shadow under it, we must be skipping and prancing about, like the beasts whom we follow.—Are we thirsty? We have nothing to drink but the waters of mountain torrents, which taste of burned stones and mawkish leaves.—Are we hungry? We must greedily devour lean venison, and that commonly roasted to a stick.—Have I a moment's repose at night?—My slumber is disturbed by the din of horses and elephants, or by the sons of slave girls hollooing out, "More venison, more venison!"—Then comes a cry that pierces my ear, "Away to the forest, away!"—Nor are these my only grievances: fresh pain is now added to the smart of my first wounds; for, while we were separated from our king, who was chasing a foolish deer, he entered, I find, yon lonely place, and there, to my infinite grief, saw a certain girl, called Sacontalá, the daughter of a hermit: from that moment not a word of returning to the city!—These distressing thoughts have kept my eyes open the whole night.—Alas! when shall we return?—I cannot set eyes on my beloved friend Dushmanta since he set his heart on taking another wife.—[*Stepping aside and looking*]—Oh! there he is.—How changed!—He carries a bow, indeed, but wears for his diadem a garland of wood-flowers.—He is advancing: I must begin my operations.—[*He stands leaning on a staff.*]—Let me thus take a moment's rest.—[*Aloud.*]

Dushmanta *enters, as described.*

Dushm. [*Aside, sighing.*] My darling is not so easily attainable; yet my heart assumes confidence from the manner in which she seemed affected: surely, though our love has not hitherto prospered, yet the inclinations of us both are fixed on our union.—[*Smiling.*]—Thus do lovers agreeably beguile themselves, when all the powers of their souls are intent on the objects of their desire!—But am I beguiled? No; when she cast her eyes even on her companions, they sparkled with tenderness; when she moved her graceful arms, they dropped, as if languid with love; when her friend remonstrated against her departure, she spoke angrily—All this was, no doubt, on my account.—Oh! how quick-sighted is love in discerning his own advantages!

Mádh. [*Bending downward, as before.*] Great prince! my hands are unable to move; and it is with my lips only that I can mutter a blessing on you. May the king be victorious!

Dushm. [*Looking at him and smiling.*] Ah! what has crippled thee, friend Mádhavya?

Mádh. You strike my eye with your own hand, and then ask what makes it weep.

Dushm. Speak intelligibly. I know not what you mean.

Mádh. Look at yon Vétas tree bent double in the river. Is it crooked, I pray, by its own act, or by the force of the stream?

Dushm. It is bent, I suppose, by the current.

Mádh. So am I by your Majesty.

Dushm. How so, Mádhavya?

Mádh. Does it become you, I pray, to leave the great affairs of your empire, and so charming a mansion as your palace, for the sake of living here like a forester? Can you hold a council in a wood? I, who am a reverend Bráhmen, have no longer the use of my hands and feet: they are put out of joint by my running all day long after dogs and wild beasts. Favor me, I entreat, with your permission to repose but a single day.

Dushm. [*Aside.*] Such are this poor fellow's complaints; whilst I, when I think of Canna's daughter, have as little relish for hunting as he. How can I brace this bow, and fix a shaft in the string, to shoot at those beautiful deer who dwell in the same groves with my beloved, and whose eyes derive lustre from hers ?

Mádh. [*Looking stedfastly at the king.*] What scheme is your royal mind contriving ? I have been crying, I find, in a wilderness.

Dushm. I think of nothing but the gratification of my old friend's wishes.

Mádh. [*Joyfully.*] Then may the king live long !

[*Rising, but counterfeiting feebleness.*

Dushm. Stay ; and listen to me attentively.

Mádh. Let the king command.

Dushm. When you have taken repose, I shall want your assistance in another business, that will give you no fatigue.

Mádh. Oh ! what can that be, unless it be eating rice-pudding ?

Dushm. You shall know in due time.

Mádh. I shall be delighted to hear it.

Dushm. Hola ! who is there ?

The Chamberlain *enters.*

Cham. Let my sovereign command me.

Dushm. Raivataca, bid the General attend.

Cham. I obey.—[*He goes out, and returns with the* General.]—Come quickly, Sir, the king stands expecting you.

Gen. [*Aside, looking at* Dushmanta.] How comes it that hunting, which moralists reckon a vice, should be a virtue in the eyes of a king ? Thence it is, no doubt, that our emperor, occupied in perpetual toil, and inured to constant heat, is become so lean, that the sunbeams hardly affect him ; while he is so tall, that he looks to us little men, like an elephant grazing on a mountain : he seems all foul.—[*Aloud, approaching the king.*] —May our monarch ever be victorious !—This forest, O king, is infested by beast of prey : we see the traces of their huge feet in every path.—What orders is it your pleasure to give ?

Dushm. Bhadraséna, this moralizing Mádhavya has put a stop to our recreation by forbidding the pleasures of the chase.

Gen. [*Aside to* Mádhavya.] Be firm to your word, my friend; whilst I sound the king's real inclinations.—[*Aloud.*] O! Sir, the fool talks idly. Consider the delights of hunting. The body, it is true, becomes emaciated, but it is light and fit for exercise. Mark how the wild beasts of various kinds are variously affected by fear and by rage! What pleasure equals that of a proud archer, when his arrow hits the mark as it flies? —Can hunting be justly called a vice? No recreation, surely, can be compared with it.

Mádh. [*Angrily.*] Away, thou false flatterer! The king, indeed, follows his natural bent, and is excusable; but thou, son of a slave girl, hast no excuse.—Away to the wood!—How I wish thou hadst been seized by a tiger or an old bear, who was prowling for a skakál, like thyself!

Dushm. We are now, Bhadraséna, encamped near a sacred hermitage; and I cannot at present applaud your panegyrick on hunting. This day, therefore, let the wild buffalos roll undisturbed in the shallow water, or toss up the sand with their horns; let the herd of antelopes, assembled under the thick shade, ruminate without fear; let the large boars root up the herbage on the brink of yon pool; and let this my bow take repose with a slackened string.

Gen. As our lord commands.

Dushm. Recall the archers who have advanced before me, and forbid the officers to go very far from this hallowed grove. Let them beware of irritating the pious: holy men are eminent for patient virtues, yet conceal within their bosoms a scorching flame; as carbuncles are naturally cool to the touch; but, if the rays of the sun have been imbibed by them, they burn the hand.

Mádh. Away now, and triumph on the delights of hunting.

Gen. The king's orders are obeyed. [*He goes out.*

Dushm. [*To his attendants.*] Put off your hunting apparel; and thou, Raivataca, continue in waiting at a little distance.

Cham. I shall obey. [*Goes out.*

Mádh. So ! you have cleared the stage : not even a fly is left on it. Sit down, I pray, on this pavement of smooth pebbles, and the shade of this tree shall be your canopy ; I will sit by you ; for I am impatient to know what will give me no fatigue.

Dushm. Go first, and seat thyself.

Mádh. Come, my royal friend. [*They both sit under a tree.*

Dushm. Friend Mádhavya, your eyes have not been gratified with an object which best deserves to be seen.

Mádh. Yes, truly ; for a king is before them.

Dushm. All men are apt, indeed, to think favorably of themselves ; but I meant Sacontalá, the brightest ornament of these woods.

Mádh. [*Aside.*] I must not foment this passion.—[*Aloud.*] What can you gain by seeing her ? She is a Bráhmen's daughter, and consequently no match for you ?

Dushm. What ! Do people gaze at the new moon, with uplifted heads and fixed eyes, from a hope of possessing it ? But you must know, that the heart of Dushmanta is not fixed on an object which he must for ever despair of attaining.

Mádh. Tell me how.

Dushm. She is the daughter of a pious prince and warrior, by a celestial nymph ; and, her mother having left her on earth, she has been fostered by Canna, even as a fresh blossom of Malati, which droops on its pendant stalk, is raised and expanded by the sun's light.

Mádh. [*Laughing.*] Your desire to possess this rustic girl, when you have women bright as gems in your palace already, is like the fancy of a man, who has lost his relish for dates, and longs for the sour tamarind.

Dushm. Did you know her, you would not talk so wildly.

Mádh. Oh ! certainly, whatever a king admires must be superlatively charming.

Dushm. [*Smiling.*] What need is there of long description ? When I meditate on the power of Brahmá, and on her lineaments, the creation of so transcendent a jewel outshines, in my apprehension, all his other works : she was formed and moulded in the eternal mind, which had raised with its utmost exertion, the ideas of perfect shapes, and thence made an assemblage of all abstract beauties.

Ma'dh. She must render, then, all other handsome women contemptible.

Dushm. In my mind she really does. I know not yet what blessed inhabitant of this world will be the possessor of that faultless beauty, which now resembles a blossom whose fragrance has not been diffused; a fresh leaf, which no hand has torn from its stalk; a pure diamond, which no polisher has handled; new honey, whose sweetness is yet untasted; or rather the celestial fruit of collected virtues, to the perfection of which nothing can be added.

Ma'dh. Make haste, then, or the fruit of all virtues will drop into the hand of some devout rustic, whose hair shines with oil of Ingudí.

Dushm. She is not her own mistress; and her foster-father is at a distance.

Ma'dh. How is she disposed towards you?

Dushm. My friend, the damsels in a hermit's family are naturally reserved; yet she did look at me, wishing to be unperceived; then she smiled, and started a new subject of conversation. Love is by nature averse to a sudden communication, and hitherto neither fully displays, nor wholly conceals, himself in her demeanour towards me.

Ma'dh. [*Laughing*] Has she thus taken possession of your heart on so transient a view?

Dushm. When she walked about with her female friends, I saw her yet more distinctly, and my passion was greatly augmented. She said sweetly, but untruly, "My foot is hurt by the points of the Cusa grass:" then she stopped; but soon, advancing a few paces, turned back her face, pretending a wish to disentangle her vest of woven bark from the branches in which it had not really been caught.

Ma'dh. You began with chasing an antelope, and have now started new game: thence it is, I presume, that you are grown so fond of a consecrated forest.

Dushm. Now the business for you, which I mentioned, is this: you, who are a Bráhmen, must find some expedient for my second entrance into that asylum of virtue.

Mádh. And the advice which I give is this: remember that you are a king.

Dushm. What then?

Mádh. "Hola! bid the hermits bring my sixth part of their grain." Say this, and enter the grove without scruple.

Dushm. No, Mádhavya: they pay a different tribute, who, having abandoned all the gems and gold of this world, possess riches far superior. The wealth of princes, collected from the four orders of their subjects, is perishable; but pious men give us a sixth part of the fruits of their piety; fruits which will never perish.

Behind the scenes.] Happy men that we are! we have now attained the object of our desire.

Dushm. Hah! I hear the voices of some religious anchorites.

The Chamberlain *enters.*

Cham. May the king be victorious!—Two young men, sons of a hermit, are waiting at my station, and soliciting an audience.

Dushm. Introduce them without delay.

Cham. As the king commands.—[*He goes out, and re-enters with two* Bráhmens.]—Come on; come this way.

First Bráhm. [*Looking at the king.*] Oh! what confidence is inspired by his brilliant appearance!—Or proceeds it rather from his disposition to virtue and holiness?——Whence comes it, that my fear vanishes?——He now has taken his abode in a wood which supplies us with every enjoyment; and with all his exertions for our safety, his devotion increases from day to day.—The praise of a monarch who has conquered his passions ascends even to heaven: inspired bards are continually singing, "Behold a virtuous prince!" but with us the royal name stands first: "Behold, among kings, a sage!"

Second Bráhm. Is this, my friend, the truly virtuous Dushmanta?

First Bráhm. Even he.

Second Bráhm. It is not then wonderful, that he alone, whose arm is lofty and strong as the main bar of his city gate, possesses the whole earth, which forms a dark boundary to the ocean; or that the gods of Swerga, who fiercely contend in battle with evil powers, proclaim victory gained by his braced bow, not by the thunderbolt of INDRA.

Both. [*Approaching him.*] O king, be victorious!

Dushm. [*Rising.*] I humbly salute you both.

Both. Blessings on thee!

Dushm. [*Respectfully.*] May I know the cause of this visit?

First Bráhm. Our sovereign is hailed by the pious inhabitants of these woods; and they implore——

Dushm. What is their command?

First Bráhm. In the absence of our spiritual guide, Canna, some evil demons are disturbing our holy retreat. Deign, therefore, accompanied by thy charioteer, to be master of our asylum, if it be only for a few short days.

Dushm. [*Eagerly.*] I am highly favored by your invitation.

Mádh. [*Aside.*] Excellent promoters of your design! They draw you by the neck, but not against your will.

Dushm. Raivataca, bid my charioteer bring my car, with my bow and quiver.

Cham. I obey. [*He goes out.*

First Bráhm. Such condescension well becomes thee, who art an universal guardian.

Second Bráhm. Thus do the descendants of Puru perform their engagement to deliver their subjects from fear of danger.

Dushm. Go first, holy men: I will follow instantly.

Both. Be ever victorious! [*They go out.*

Dushm. Shall you not be delighted, friend Mádhavya, to see my Sacontalá?

Mádh. At first I should have had no objection; but I have a considerable one since the story of the demons.

Dushm. Oh! fear nothing: you will be near me.

Mádh. And you, I hope, will have leisure to protect me from them.

The Chamberlain *re-enters.*

Cham. May our lord be victorious!—The imperial car is ready; and all are expecting your triumphant approach. Carabba too, a messenger from the queen-mother, is just arrived from the city.

Dushm. Is he really come from the venerable queen?

Cham. There can be no doubt of it.

Dushm. Let him appear before me.

[*The* Chamberlain *goes out, and returns with the* Messenger.

Cham. There stands the king—O Carabba, approach him with reverence.

Mess. [*Prostrating himself.*] May the king be ever victorious!—The royal mother sends this message——

Dushm. Declare her command.

Mess. Four days hence the usual fast for the advancement of her son will be kept with solemnity; and the presence of the king (may his life be prolonged!) will then be required.

Dushm. On one hand is a commission from holy Bráhmens; on the other, a command from my revered parent: both duties are sacred, and neither must be neglected.

Mádh. [*Laughing.*] Stay suspended between them both, like king Trisancu between heaven and earth; when the pious men said, "Rise!" and the gods of Swerga said, "Fall!"

Dushm. In truth I am greatly perplexed. My mind is principally distracted by the distance of the two places where the two duties are to be performed; as the stream of a river is divided by rocks in the middle of its bed.—[*Musing.*]—Friend Mádhavya, my mother brought you up as her own son, to be my playfellow, and to divert me in my childhood. You may very properly act my part in the queen's devotions. Return then to the city, and give an account of my distress through the commission of these reverend foresters.

D

Mádh. That I will;—but you could not really suppose that I was afraid of demons!

Dushm. How come you, who are an egregious Bráhmen, to be so bold on a sudden?

Mádh. Oh! I am now a young king.

Dushm. Yes, certainly; and I will dispatch my whole train to attend your highness, whilst I put an end to the disturbance in this hermitage.

Mádh. [*Strutting.*] See, I am a prince regnant.

Dushm. [*Aside.*] This buffoon of a Bráhmen has a slippery genius. He will perhaps disclose my present pursuit to the women in the palace. I must try to deceive him.—[*Taking* Mádhavya *by the hand.*]—I shall enter the forest, be assured, only through respect for its pious inhabitants; not from any inclination for the daughter of a hermit. How far am I raised above a girl educated among antelopes; a girl, whose heart must ever be a stranger to love!—The tale was invented for my diversion.

Mádh. Yes, to be sure; only for yonr diversion!

Dushm. Then farewel, my friend; execute my commission faithfully, whilst I proceed——to defend the anchorites.

[*All go out.*

ACT III.

SCENE—*The* HERMITAGE *in a Grove.*

The Hermit's Pupil *bearing consecrated grass.*

Pupil [*Meditating with wonder.*]

HOW great is the power of Dushmanta!—The monarch and his charioteer had no sooner entered the grove than we continued our holy rites without interruption.—What words can describe him?—By his barely aiming a shaft, by the mere sound of his bow-string, by the simple murmur of his vibrating bow, he disperses at once our calamities.—Now then I deliver to the priests this bundle of fresh Cusa grass to be scattered round the place of sacrifice.——[*Looking behind the scenes.*]—Ah! Priyamvadá, for whom are you carrying that ointment of Usíra root, and those leaves of water lilies?—[*Listening attentively.*]—What say you?—That Sacontalá is extremely disordered by the sun's heat, and that you have procured for her a cooling medicine!—Let her, my Priyamvadá, be diligently attended; for she is the darling of our venerable father Canna.—I will administer, by the hand of Gautamí, some healing water consecrated in the ceremony called Vaitána. [*He goes out.*

Dushmanta *enters, expressing the distraction of a lover.*

Dushm. I well know the power of her devotion: that she will suffer none to dispose of her but Canna, I too well know. Yet my heart can no more return to its former placid state, than water can reascend the steep, down which it has fallen.—O God of Love, how can thy darts be so keen, since they are pointed with flowers?—Yes, I discover the reason of their keenness. They are tipped with the flames which the wrath of Hara kindled, and which blaze at this moment, like the Bárava fire under the waves: how else couldst thou, who wast consumed even to ashes, be still the inflamer of our souls? By thee and by the moon, though each of you seems worthy of confidence, we lovers are cruelly deceived. They who love as I do, ascribe flowery shafts to thee, and cool beams to the moon, with equal impropriety; for the moon sheds fire on them with her dewy rays, and thou pointest with sharp diamonds those arrows which seem to be barbed with blossoms. Yet this god, who bears a fish on his banners, and who wounds me to the soul, will give me real delight, if he destroy me with the aid of my beloved, whose eyes are large and beautiful as those of a roe.——O powerful divinity, even when I thus adore thy attributes, hast thou no compassion? Thy fire, O Love, is fanned into a blaze by a hundred of my vain thoughts.—Does it become thee to draw thy bow even to thy ear, that the shaft, aimed at my bosom, may inflict a deeper wound?—Where now can I recreate my afflicted soul by the permission of those pious men whose uneasiness I have removed by dismissing my train?—[*Sighing.*]—I can have no relief but from a sight of my beloved.——[*Looking up.*]—This intensely hot noon must, no doubt, be passed by Sacontalá with her damsels on the banks of this river over-shadowed with Tamálas.—It must be so:—I will advance thither.—[*Walking round and looking.*]—My sweet friend has, I guess, been lately walking under that row of young trees; for I see the stalks of some flowers, which probably she gathered, still unshrivelled; and some fresh leaves, newly plucked, still dropping milk.——[*Feeling a breeze.*—Ah! this bank has a delightful air!—Here may the gale embrace me, wasting odours from the water lilies, and cool my breast, inflamed by the bodiless god, with the liquid particles which it catches from the waves of the Málinì.—[*Looking down.*] —Happy lover! Sacontalá must be somewhere in this grove of flowering creepers; for I discern on the yellow sand at the door of yon arbour some recent footsteps, raised a little before, and depressed behind by the weight of her elegant limbs.—I shall have a better view from behind this thick foliage.—[*He conceals himself, looking vigilantly.*]—Now are my eyes fully gratified.—The darling of my heart, with her two faithful attendants, reposes on a smooth rock strown with fresh flowers.—These branches will hide me, whilst I hear their charming conversation. [*He stands concealed, and gazes.*

Sacontalá *and her two Damsels discovered.*

Both. [*Fanning her.*] Say, beloved Sacontalá, does the breeze, raised by our fans of broad lotos leaves, refresh you?

Sac. [*Mournfully.*] Why, alas, do my dear friends take this trouble? [*Both look sorrowfully at each other.*

Dushm. [*Aside.*] Ah! she seems much indisposed. What can have been the fatal cause of so violent a fever?—Is it what my heart suggests? Or—[*Musing*]—I am perplexed with doubts.—The medicine extracted from the balmy Usíra has been applied, I see, to her bosom: her only bracelet is made of thin filaments from the stalks of a water lily, and even that is loosely bound on her arm. Yet, even thus disordered, she is exquisitely beautiful.—Such are the hearts of the young! Love and the sun equally inflame us; but the scorching heat of summer leads not equally to happiness with the ardour of youthful desires.

Pri. [*Aside to* Anusúyá.] Did you not observe how the heart of Sacontalá was affected by the first sight of our pious monarch? My suspicion is, that her malady has no other cause.

Anu. [*Aside to* Priyamvadá.] The same suspicion had risen in my mind. I will ask her at once.—[*Aloud*]—My sweet Sacontalá, let me put one question to you. What has really occasioned your indisposition?

Dushm. [*Aside.*] She must now declare it. Ah! though her bracelets of lotos are bright as moon beams, yet they are marked, I see, with black spots from internal ardour.

Sac. [*Half raising herself.*] Oh! say what you suspect to have occasioned it.

Anu. Sacontalá, we must necessarily be ignorant of what is passing in your breast; but I suspect your case to be that which we have often heard related in tales of love. Tell us openly what causes your illness. A physician, without knowing the cause of a disorder, cannot even begin to apply a remedy.

Dushm. [*Aside.*] I flatter myself with the same suspicion.

Sac. [*Aside.*] My pain is intolerable ; yet I cannot hastily disclose the occasion of it.

Pri. My sweet friend, Anusúyá, speaks rationally. Consider the violence of your indisposition. Every day you will be more and more emaciated, though your exquisite beauty has not yet forsaken you.

Dushm. [*Aside.*] Most true. Her forehead is parched ; her neck droops ; her waist is more slender than before ; her shoulders languidly fall ; her complection is wan ; she resembles a Mádhaví creeper, whose leaves are dried by a sultry gale : yet, even thus transformed, she is lovely, and charms my soul.

Sac. [*Sighing.*] What more can I say ? Ah ! why should I be the occasion of your sorrow ?

Pri. For that very reason, my beloved, we are solicitous to know your secret ; since, when each of us has a share of your uneasiness, you will bear more easily your own portion of it.

Dushm. [*Aside.*] Thus urged by two friends, who share her pains as well as her pleasures, she cannot fail to disclose the hidden cause of her malady ; whilst I, on whom she looked at our first interview with marked affection, am filled with anxious desire to hear her answer.

Sac. From the very instant when the accomplished prince, who has just given repose to our hallowed forest, met my eye——

[*She breaks off, and looks modest*

Both. Speak on, beloved Sacontalá,

Sac. From that instant my affection was unalterably fixed on him—and thence I am reduced to my present languor.

Anu. Fortunately your affection is placed on a man worthy of yourself.

Pri. Oh! could a fine river have deserted the sea and flowed into a lake ?

Dushm. [*Joyfully.*] That which I was eager to know, her own lips have told. Love was the cause of my distemper, and love has healed it ; as a summer's day, grown black with clouds, relieves all animals from the heat which itself had caused,

Sac. If it be no disagreeable task, contrive, I entreat you, some means by which I may find favor in the king's eyes

Dushm. [*Aside.*] That request banishes all my cares, and gives me rapture even in my present situation.

Pri. [*Aside to* Anusúyá.] A remedy for her, my friend, will scarce be attainable. Exert all the powers of your mind; for her illness admits of no delay.

Ánu. [*Aside to* Priyamvadá.] By what expedient can her cure be both accelerated and kept secret?

Pri. [*As before.*] Oh! to keep it secret will be easy; but to attain it soon, almost insuperably difficult.

Anu. [*As before.*] How so?

Pri. The young king seemed, I admit, by his tender glances, to be enamoured of her at first sight; and he has been observed, within these few days, to be pale and thin, as if his passion had kept him long awake.

Dushm. [*Aside.*] So it has——This golden bracelet, sullied by the flame which preys on me, and which no dew mitigates, but the tears gushing nightly from these eyes, has fallen again and again on my wrist, and has been replaced on my emaciated arm.

Pri. [*Aloud.*] I have a thought, Anusúyá—Let us write a love letter, which I will conceal in a flower, and, under the pretext of making a respectful offering, deliver it myself into the king's hand.

Anu. An excellent contrivance! It pleases me highly;—but what says our beloved Sacontalá?

Sac. I must consider, my friend, the possible consequences of such a step.

Pri. Think also of a verse or two, which may suit your passion, and be consistent with the character of a lovely girl born in an exalted family.

Sac. I will think of them in due time; but my heart flutters with the apprehension of being rejected.

Dushm. [*Aside.*] Here stands the man supremely blessed in thy presence, from whom, O timid girl, thou art apprehensive of a refusal! Here stands the man, from whom, O beautiful maid, thou fearest rejection, though he loves thee distractedly. He who shall possess thee will seek no brighter gem; and thou art the gem which I am eager to possess.

Anu. You depreciate, Sacontalá, your own incomparable merits. What man in his senses would intercept with an umbrella the moonlight of autumn, which alone can allay the fever caused by the heat of the noon?

Sac. [*Smiling.*] I am engaged in thought. [*She meditates.*

Dushm. Thus then I fix my eyes on the lovely poetess, without closing them a moment, while she measures the feet of her verse: her forehead is gracefully moved in cadence, and her whole aspect indicates pure affection.

Sac. I have thought of a couplet; but we have no writing implements.

Pri. Let us hear the words; and then I will mark them with my nail on this lotos leaf, soft and green as the breast of a young parroquet: it may easily be cut into the form of a letter.— Repeat the verses.

Sac. "Thy heart, indeed, I know not: but mine, oh! cruel, love warms by day and by night; and all my faculties are centered on thee."

Dushm. [*Hastily advancing, and pronouncing a verse in the same measure.*] "Thee, O slender maid, love only warms; but me he burns; as the day-star only stifles the fragrance of the night-flower, but quenches the very orb of the moon."

Anu. [*Looking at him joyfully.*] Welcome, great king; the fruit of my friend's imagination has ripened without delay.

[Sacontalà *expresses an inclination to rise.*

Dushm. Give yourself no pain. Those delicate limbs, which repose on a couch of flowers, those arms, whose bracelets of lotos are disarranged by a slight pressure, and that sweet frame, which the hot noon seems to have disordered, must not be fatigued by ceremony.

Sac. [*Aside.*] O my heart, canst thou not rest at length after all thy sufferings?

Anu. Let our sovereign take for his seat a part of the rock on which she reposes. [Sacontalá *makes a little room.*

Dushm. [*Seating himself.*] Priyamvadá, is not the fever of your charming friend in some degree abated ?

Pri. [*Smiling*] She has just taken a salutary medicine, and will soon be restored to health. But O mighty prince, as I am favored by you and by her, my friendship for Sacontalá prompts me to converse with you for a few moments.

Dushm. Excellent damsel, speak openly ; and suppress nothing.

Pri. Our lord shall hear.

Dushm. I am attentive.

Pri. By dispelling the alarms of our pious hermits, you have discharged the duty of a great monarch.

Dushm. Oh ! talk a little on other subjects.

Pri. Then I must inform yon that our beloved companion is enamoured of you, and has been reduced to her present languor by the resistless divinity, love. You only can preserve her inestimable life.

Dushm. Sweet Priyamvadá, our passion is reciprocal ; but it is I who am honored.

Sac. [*Smiling, with a mixture of affection and resentment.*] Why should you detain the virtuous monarch, who must be afflicted by so long an absence from the secret apartments of his palace ?

Dushm. This heart of mine, oh thou who art of all things the dearest to it, will have no object but thee, whose eyes enchant me with their black splendour, if thou wilt but speak in a milder strain. I, who was nearly slain by love's arrow, am destroyed by thy speech.

Anu. [*Laughing.*] Princes are said to have many fovorite consorts. You must assure us, therefore, that our beloved friend shall not be exposed to affliction through our conduct.

Dushm. What need is there of many words ? Let there be ever so many women in my palace, I will have only two objects of perfect regard; the sea-girt earth, which I govern, and your sweet friend, whom I love.

Both. Our anxiety is dissipated.

[Sacontalá *strives in vain to conceal her joy.*

Pri. [*Aside to* Anusúyá.] See how our friend recovers her spirits by little and little, as the peahen, oppressed by the summer heat, is refreshed by a soft gale and a gentle shower.

Sac. [*To the damsels.*] Forgive, I pray, my offence in having used unmeaning words: they were uttered only for your amusement in return for your tender care of me.

Pri. They were the occasion, indeed, of our serious advice. But it is the king who must forgive: who else is offended?

Sac. The great monarch will, I trust, excuse what has been said either before him or in his absence.—[*Aside to the damsels.*] Intercede with him, I entreat you.

Dushm. [*Smiling.*] I would cheerfully forgive any offence, lovely Sacontalá, if you, who have dominion over my heart, would allow me full room to sit by you, and recover from my fatigue, on this flowery couch pressed by your delicate limbs.

Pri. Allow him room; it will appease him, and make him happy.

Sac. [*Pretending anger, aside to* Priyamadá.] Be quiet, thou mischief-making girl! Dost thou sport with me in my present weak state?

Anu. [*Looking behind the scenes.*] O! my Priyamvadá, there is our favorite young antelope running wildly and turning his eyes on all sides: he is no doubt, seeking his mother, who has rambled in the wide forest. I must go and assist his search.

Pri. He is very nimble; and you alone will never be able to confine him in one place. I must accompany you.

[*Both going out.*

Sac. Alas! I cannot consent to your going far: I shall be left alone.

Both. [*Smiling.*] Alone! with the sovereign of the world by your side! [*They go out.*

Sac. How could my companions both leave me ?

[*Dushm.* Sweet maid, give yourself no concern. Am not I, who humbly solicit your favor, present in the room of them ?—[*Aside.*]—I must declare my passion.——[*Aloud.*]—Why should not I, like them wave this fan of lotos leaves, to raise cool breezes and dissipate your uneasiness ? Why should not I, like them, lay softly in my lap those feet, red as water lilies, and press them, O my charmer, to relieve your pain ?

Sac. I should offend against myself, by receiving homage from a person entitled to my respect.

[*She rises, and walks slowly through weakness.*

Dushm. The noon, my love, is not yet passed ; and your sweet limbs are weak. Having left that couch where fresh flowers covered your bosom, you can ill sustain this intense heat with so languid a frame. [*He gently draws her back.*

Sac. Leave me, oh leave me. I am not, indeed, my own mistress, or——the two damsels were only appointed to attend me. What can I do at present ?

Dushm. [*Aside*] Fear of displeasing her makes me bashful.

Sac. [*Overhearing him*] The king cannot give offence. It is my unhappy fate only that I accuse.

Dushm. Why should you accuse so favorable a destiny ?

Sac. How rather can I help blaming it, since it has permitted my heart to be affected by amiable qualities, without having left me at my own disposal ?

Dushm. [*Aside.*] One would imagine that the charming sex, instead of being, like us, tormented with love, kept love himself within their hearts, to torment him with delay.

[Sacontalá *going out.*

Dushm. [*Aside.*] How! must I then fail of attaining felicity ? [*Following her and catching the skirt of her mantle.*

Sac. [*Turning back.*] Son of Puru, preserve thy reason ; oh! preserve it.—The hermits are busy on all sides of the grove.

Dushm. My charmer, your fear of them is vain. Canna himself, who is deeply versed in the science of law, will be no obstacle to our union. Many daughters of the holiest men have been married by the ceremony called Gándharva, as it is practised by Indra's band, and even their fathers have approved them.—[*Looking round.*]—What say you? are you still inflexible? Alas! I must then depart.

[*Going from her a few paces, then looking back.*

Sac. [*Moving also a few steps, and then turning back her face.*] Though I have refused compliance, and have only allowed you to converse with me for a moment, yet, O son of Puru—let not Sacontalá be wholly forgotten.

Dushm. Enchanting girl, should you be removed to the ends of the world, you will be fixed in this heart, as the shade of a lofty tree remains with it even when the day is departed.

Sac. [*Going out, aside.*] Since I have heard his protestations, my feet move, indeed, but without advancing. I will conceal myself behind those flowering Curuvacas, and thence I shall see the result of his passion.

[*She hides herself behind the shrubs.*

Dushm. [*Aside.*] Can you leave me, beloved Sacontalá; me who am all affection ? Could you not have tarried a single moment ? Soft is your beautiful frame, and indicates a benevolent soul ; yet your heart is obdurate : as the tender Siríshа hangs on a hard stalk.

Sac. [*Aside.*] I really have now lost the power of departing.

Dushm. [*Aside.*] What can I do in this retreat since my darling has left it ?—[*Musing and looking round.*]—Ah ! my departure is happily delayed.—Here lies her bracelet of flowers, exquisitely perfumed by the root of Usíra which had been spread on her bosom : it has fallen from her delicate wrist, and is become a new chain for my heart.

[*Taking up the bracelet with reverence.*

Sac. [*Aside, looking at her hand.*] Ah me ! such was my languor, that the filaments of lotos stalks which bound my arm dropped on the ground unperceived by me.

Dushm. [*Aside, placing it in his bosom.*] Oh ! how delightful to the touch !—From this ornament of your lovely arm, O my darling, though it be inanimate and senseless, your unhappy lover has regained confidence—a bliss which you refused to confer.

Sac. [*Aside.*] I can stay here no longer. By this pretext I may return. [*Going slowly towards him.*

Dushm. [*With rapture.*] Ah! the empress of my soul again blesses these eyes. After all my misery I was destined to be favored by indulgent heaven.—The bird Chátac, whose throat was parched with thirst, supplicated for a drop of water, and suddenly a cool stream poured into his bill from the bounty of a fresh cloud.

Sac. Mighty king, when I had gone half way to the cottage, I perceived that my bracelet of thin stalks had fallen from my wrist; and I return because my heart is almost convinced that you must have seen and taken it. Restore it, I humbly entreat, lest you expose both yourself and me to the censure of the hermits.

Dushm. Yes, on one condition I will return it.

Sac. On what condition? Speak——

Dushm. That I may replace it on the wrist to which it belongs.

Sac. [*Aside.*] I have no alternative. [*Approaching him.*

Dushm. But in order to replace it, we must both be seated on that smooth rock. [*Both sit down.*

Dushm. [*Taking her hand.*] O exquisite softness! This hand has regained its native strength and beauty, like a young shoot of Cámalatá: or it resembles rather the god of love himself, when, having been consumed by the fire of Hara's wrath, he was restored to life by a shower of nectar sprinkled by the immortals.

Sac. [*Pressing his hand.*] Let the son of my lord make haste to tie on the bracelet.

Dushm. [*Aside, with rapture.*] Now I am truly blessed.—That phrase, the son of my lord, is applied only to a husband.—[*Aloud.*]—My charmer, the clasp of this bracelet is not easily loosened: it must be made to fit you better.

Sac. [*Smiling.*] As you please.

Dushm. [*Quitting her hand.*] Look, my darling: this is the new moon which left the firmament in honor of superior beauty, and, having descended on your enchanting wrist, has joined both its horns round it in the shape of a bracelet.

Sac. I really see nothing like a moon: the breeze, I suppose, has shaken some dust from the lotos flower behind my ears, and that has obscured my sight.

Dushm. [*Smiling.*] If you permit me, I will blow the fragrant dust from your eye.

Sac. It would be a kindness; but I cannot trust you.

Dushm. Oh! fear not, fear not. A new servant never transgresses the command of his mistress.

Sac. But a servant over-assiduous deserves no confidence.

Dushm. [*Aside.*] I will not let slip this charming occasion. ——[*Attempting to raise her head*—Sacontalá *faintly repels him, but sits still.*]——O damsel with an antelope's eyes be not apprehensive of my indiscretion.——[Sacontalá *looks up for a moment, and then bashfully drops her head*—Dushmanta, *aside, gently raising her head.*]——That lip, the softness of which is imagined, not proved, seems to pronounce, with a delightful tremour, its permission for me to allay my thirst.

Sac. The son of my lord seems inclined to break his promise.

Dushm. Beloved, I was deceived by the proximity of the lotos to that eye which equals it in brightness.

[*He blows gently on her eye.*

Sac. Well; now I see a prince who keeps his word as it becomes his imperial character. Yet I am really ashamed that no desert of mine entitles me to the kind service of my lord's son.

Dushm. What reward can I desire, except that which I consider as the greatest, the fragrance of your delicious lip?

Sac. Will that content you?

Dushm. The bee is contented with the mere odour of the water lily.

Sac. If he were not, he would get no remedy.

[*Kissing her eagerly.*

Dushm. Yes, this and this——

Behind the scenes. Hark ! the Chacraváca is calling her mate on the bank of the Máliní : the night is beginning to spread her shades.

Sac. [*Listening alarmed.*] O son of my lord, the matron Gautami approaches to enquire after my health. Hide yourself, I entreat, behind yon trees.

Dushm. I yield to necessity. [*He retires.*

Gautamí *enters with a vase in her hand.*

Gaut. [*Looking anxiously at* Sacontalá.] My child, here is holy water for thee.—What ! hast thou no companion here but the invisible gods ; thou who art so much indisposed ?

Sac. Both Priyamvadá and Anusùyá are just gone down to the river.

Gaut. [*Sprinkling her.*] Is thy fever, my child, a little abated ? [*Feeling her hand.*

Sac. Venerable matron, there is a change for the better.

Gaut. Then thou art in no danger. Mayst thou live many years ! The day is departing : let us both go to the cottage.

Sac. [*Aside, rising slowly.*] O my heart, no sooner hadst thou begun to taste happiness, than the occasion slipped away !—[*She advances a few steps, and returns to the arbour.*]—O bower of twining plants, by whom my sorrows have been dispelled, on thee I call ; ardently hoping to be once more happy under thy shade. [*She goes out with* Gautamí.

Dushm. [*Returning to the bower, and sighing.*] How, alas, have my desires been obstructed !—Could I do less than kiss the lips of my charmer, though her modest cheeks were half averted ; lips, whose sweetness had enchanted me, even when they pronounced a denial ?—Whither now can I go ?—I will remain a while in this arbour of creepers, which my darling's presence has illuminated.——[*Looking round.*]—Yes ; this is her seat on the rock, spread with blossoms, which have been pressed by her delicate limbs.—Here lies her exquisite love letter on the leaf of a water lily ; here lay her bracelet of tender filaments which had fallen from her sweet wrist.—Though the bower of twining Vétasas be now desolate, since my charmer has left it, yet, while my eyes are fixed on all these delightful memorials of her, I am unable to depart.——[*Musing.*]—Ah ! how imperfectly has this affair been conducted by a lover, like me, who, with his darling by his side, has let the occasion slip.—Should Sacontalá visit once more this calm retreat, the opportunity shall not pass again unimproved: the pleasures of youth are by nature transitory.—Thus my foolish heart forms resolutions, while it is distracted by the sudden interruption of its happiness. Why did it ever allow me to quit without effect the presence of my beloved ?

Behind the scenes. O king, while we are beginning our evening sacrifice, the figures of blood-thirsty demons, embrowned by clouds collected at the departure of day, glide over the sacred hearth, and spread consternation around.

Dushm. Fear not, holy men.—Your king will protect you.

[*He goes out.*

ACT IV.

SCENE—*A* LAWN *before the Cottage.*

The two damsels are discovered gathering flowers.

Anusúyá.

O MY Priyamvadá, though our sweet friend has been happily married, according to the rites of Gandharvas, to a bridegroom equal in rank and accomplishments, yet my affectionate heart is not wholly free from care; and one doubt gives me particular uneasiness.

Pri. What doubt, my Anusúyá ?

Anu. This morning the pious prince was dismissed with gratitude by our hermits, who had then completed their mystic rites: he is now gone to his capital, Hastinápura, where, surrounded by a hundred women in the recesses of his palace, it may be doubted whether he will remember his charming bride.

Pri. In that respect you may be quite easy. Men, so well informed and well educated as he, can never be utterly destitute of honor.—We have another thing to consider. When our father Canna shall return from his pilgrimage, and shall hear what has passed, I cannot tell how he may receive the intelligence.

Anu. If you ask my opinion, he will, I think, approve of the marriage.

Pri. Why do you think so ?

Anu. Because he could desire nothing better, than that a husband so accomplished and so exalted should take Sacontalá by the hand. It was, you know, the declared object of his heart, that she might be suitably married; and, since heaven has done for him what he most wished to do, how can he possibly be dissatisfied ?

Pri. You reason well; but—[*Looking at her basket.*]—My friend, we have plucked a sufficient store of flowers to scatter over the place of sacrifice.

F

Anu. Let us gather more to decorate the temples of the goddesses who have procured for Sacontalá so much good fortune.

[*They both gather more flowers.*

Behind the scenes. It is I——Hola!

Anu. [*Listening.*] I hear the voice, as it seems, of a guest arrived in the hermitage.

Pri. Let us hasten thither. Sacontalà is now reposing; but though we may, when she wakes, enjoy her presence, yet her mind will all day be absent with her departed lord.

Anu. Be it so; but we have occasion, you know, for all these flowers. [*They advance.*

Again behind the scenes. How! Dost thou show no attention to a guest? Then hear my imprecations——" He on whom thou art meditating, on whom alone thy heart is now fixed, while thou neglectest a pure gem of devotion who demands hospitality, shall forget thee, when thou seest him next, as a man restored to sobriety forgets the words which he uttered in a state of intoxication."

[*Both damsels look at each other with affliction.*

Pri. Wo is me! Dreadful calamity! Our beloved friend has, through mere absence of mind, provoked by her neglect, some holy man who expected reverence.

Anu. [*Looking.*] It must be so; for the choleric Durvásas is going hastily back.

Pri. Who else has power to consume, like raging fire, whatever offends him? Go, my Anusúyá; fall at his feet, and persuade him, if possible, to return: in the mean time I will prepare water and refreshments for him.

Anu. I go with eagerness. [*She goes out.*

Pri. [*Advancing hastily, her foot slips.*] Ah! through my eager haste I have let the basket fall; and my religious duties must not be postponed. [*She gathers fresh flowers.*

Anusúyá *re-enters.*

Anu. His wrath, my beloved, passes all bounds. Who living could now appease him by the humblest prostration or entreaties? yet at last he a little relented.

Pri. That little is a great deal for him.—But inform me how you soothed him in any degree.

Anu. When he positively refused to come back, I threw myself at his feet, and thus addressed him : " Holy sage, forgive I entreat, the offence of an amiable girl, who has the highest veneration for you, but was ignorant, through distraction of mind, how exalted a personage was calling to her.

Pri. What then ? What said he ?

Anu. He answered thus : My word must not be recalled ; but the spell which it has raised shall be wholly removed when her lord shall see his ring," Saying this, he disappeared.

Pri. We may now have confidence ; for before the monarch departed, he fixed with his own hand on the finger of Sacontalá the ring, on which we saw the name Dushmanta engraved, and which we will instantly recognize. On him therefore alone will depend the remedy for our misfortune.

Anu. Come, let us now proceed to the shrines of the goddesses, and implore their succour. [*Both advance.*

Pri. [*Looking.*] See, my Anusúyá, where our beloved friend sits, motionless as a picture, supporting her languid head with her left hand. With a mind so intent on one object, she can pay no attention to herself, much less to a stranger.

Anu. Let the horrid imprecation, Priyamvadá, remain a secret between us two : we must spare the feelings of our beloved, who is naturally susceptible of quick emotions.

Pri. Who would pour boiling water on the blossom of a tender Mallicá ? [*Both go out.*

A Pupil *of* Canna *enters.*

Pup. I am ordered by the venerable Canna, who is returned from the place of his pilgrimage, to observe the time of the night, and am, therefore, come forth to see how much remains of it.—[*Walking round, and observing the heavens.*]—On one side, the moon, who kindles the flowers of the Oshadhi, has nearly sunk in his western bed ; and, on the other, the sun seated behind his charioteer Arun, is beginning his course : the lustre of them both is conspicuous, when they rise and when they set ; and by their example should men be equally firm in prosperous and in adverse fortune.—The moon has now disappeared, and the night flower pleases no more ; it leaves only a remembrance of its odour, and languishes like a tender bride whose pain is intolerable in the absense of her beloved.—The ruddy morn impurples the dew drops on the branches of yonder Vadarí ; the peacock, shaking off sleep, hastens from the cottages of hermits interwoven with holy grass ; and yonder antelope, springing hastily from the place of sacrifice, which is marked with his hoofs, raises, himself on high, and stretches, his graceful limbs.—How is the moon fallen from the sky with diminished beams ! the moon who had set his foot on the head of Suméru, king of mountains, and had climed, scattering the rear of darkness, even to the central palace of Vishnu !—Thus do the great men of this world ascend with extreme labor to the summit of ambition, but easily and quickly descend from it.

Anusúyá *enters meditating.*

Anu. [*Aside.*] Such has been the affection of Sacontalá, though she was bred in austere devotion, averse from sensual enjoyments—How unkind was the king to leave her !

Pup. [*Aside.*] The proper time is come for performing the hóma : I must apprise our preceptor of it. [*He goes out.*

Anu. The shades of night are dispersed ; and I am hardly awake ; but where I ever so perfectly in my senses, what could I now do ? My hands move not readily to the usual occupations of the morning.—Let the blame be cast on love only by whom our friend has been reduced to her present condition, through a monarch who has broken his word —Or does the imprecation of Durvásas already prevail ?—How else could a virtuous king, who made so solemn an engagement, have suffered so long a time to elapse without sending even a message ?—Shall we convey the fatal ring to him ?—Or what expedient can be suggested for the relief of this incomparable girl, who mourns without ceasing ?—Yet what fault has she committed ?—With all my zeal for her happiness, I cannot summon courage enough to inform our father Canna that she is pregnant.—What then, oh ! what step can I take to relieve her anxiety ?

Priyamvadá *enters.*

Pri. Come, Anusúyá, come quickly. They are making suitable preparations for conducting Sacontalá to her husband's palace.

Anu. [*With surprise.*] What say you, my friend ?

Pri. Hear me. I went just now to Sacontalá, meannig only to ask if she had slept well—

Anu. What then ? oh ! what then ?

Pri. She was sitting with her head bent on her knee, when our father Canna, entering her apartment, embraced and congratulated her.—" My sweet child, " said he, " there has been a happy omen : the young Bráhmen who officiated in our morning sacrifice, though his sight was impeded by clouds of smoke, dropped the clarified butter into the very centre of the adorable flame.—Now, since the pious act of my pupil has prospered, my foster child must not be suffered any longer to languish in sorrow ; and this day I am determined to send thee from the cottage of the old hermit who bred thee up, to the palace of the monarch who has taken thee by the hand."

Anu. My friend, who told Canna what passed in his absence ?

Pri. When he entered the place where the holy fire was blazing he heard a voice from heaven pronouncing divine measures.—

Anu. [*Amazed.*] Ah ! you astonish me.

Pri. Hear the celestial verse:—" Know that thy adopted daughter, O pious Bráhmen, has received from Dushmanta a ray of glory destined to rule the world ; as the wood Samì becomes pregnant with mysterious fire."

Anu. [*Embracing* Priyamvadá.] I am delighted, my beloved ; I am transported with joy. But—since they mean to deprive us of our friend so soon as to-day, I feel that my delight is at least equalled by my sorrow.

Pri. Oh! we must submit patiently to the anguish of parting. Our beloved friend will now be happy ; and that should console us.

Anu. Let us now make haste to dress her in bridal array. I have already, for that purpose, filled the shell of a cocoanut, which you see fixed on an Amra tree, with the fragrant dust of Nágacésaras : take it down, and keep it in a fresh lotos leaf, whilst I collect some Góráchana from the forehead of a sacred Cow, some earth from consecrated ground, and some fresh Cusa grass, of which I will make a paste to ensure good fortune.

Pri. By all means. [*She takes down the perfume.*—Anusúyá *goes out.*

Behind the scenes. O Gautamí, bid the two Misras, Sàrngarava and Sáradwata, make ready to accompany my child Sacontalá.

Pri. [*Listening.*] Lose no time, Anusúyá, lose no time. Our father Canna is giving orders for the intended journey to Hastinápura.

Anusúyá *re-enters with the ingredients of her charm.*

Anu. I am here : let us go, my Priyamvadá.

[*They both advance.*

Pri. [*Looking.*] There stands our Sacontalá, after her bath at sunrise, while many holy women, who are congratulating her, carry baskets of hallowed grain.—Let us hasten to greet her.

Enter Sacontalá, Gautamí, *and female Hermits.*

Sac. I prostrate myself before the goddess.

Gaut. My child, thou canst not pronounce too often the word goddess : thus wilt thou procure great felicity for thy lord.

Herm. Mayst thou, O royal bride, be delivered of a hero !

[*The* Hermits *go out.*

Both damsels. [*Approaching* Sacontalá.] Beloved friend, was your bath pleasant ?

Sac. O ! my friends, you are welcome : let us sit a while together. [*They seat themselves.*

Anu. Now you must be patient, whilst I bind on a charm to secure your happiness.

Sac. That is kind.—Much has been decided this day: and the pleasure of being thus attended by my sweet friends will not soon return. [*Wiping off her tears.*

Pri. Beloved, it is unbecoming to weep at a time when you are going to be so happy.—[*Both damsels burst into tears as they dress her.*]—Your elegant person deserves richer apparel it is now decorated with such rude flowers as we could procure in this forest.

Canna's Pupil *enters with rich clothes.*

Pup. Here is a complete dress. Let the queen wear it auspiciously; and may her life be long! [*The women look with astonishmement.*

Gaut. My son, Hárita, whence came this apparel?

Pup. From the devotion of our father Canna.

Gaut. What dost thou mean?

Pup. Be attentive. The venerable sage gave this order: "Bring fresh flowers for Sacontalá from the most beautiful trees;" and suddenly the woodnymphs appeared raising their hands, which rivalled new leaves in beauty and softness. Some of them wove a lower mantle bright as the moon, the presage of her felicity; another pressed the juice of Lácshá to stain her feet exquisitely red; the rest were busied in forming the gayest ornaments; and they eagerly showered their gifts on us.

Pri. [*Looking at* Sacontalá.] Thus it is, that even the bee, whose nest is within the hollow trunk, does homage to the honey of the lotos flower.

Gaut. The nymphs must have been commissioned by the goddess of the king's fortune, to predict the accession of brighter ornaments in his palace. [Sacontalá *looks modest.*

Pup. I must hasten to Canna, who is gone to bathe in the Màlinì, and let him know the signal kindness of the woodnymphs. [*He goes out.*

Anu. My sweet friend, I little expected so splendid a dress:—how shall I adjust it properly?—[*Considering.*]—Oh!

my skill in painting will supply me with some hints; and I will dispose the drapery acccording to art.

Sac. I well know your affection for him.

Canna *enters meditating.*

Can. [*Aside.*] This day must Sacontalá depart: that is resolved; yet my soul is smitten with anguish.—My speech is interrupted by a torrent of tears, which my reason suppresses and turns inward: my very sight is dimmed.—Strange that the affliction of a forester, retired from the haunts of men, should be so excessive!—Oh, with what pangs must they who are fathers of families, be afflicted on the departure of a daughter!

[*He walks round musing.*

Pri. Now, my Sacontalá, you are becomingly decorated: put on this lower vest the gift of sylvan goddesses.

[Sacontalá *rises and puts on the mantle.*

Gaut. My child, thy spiritual father, whose eyes overflow with tears of joy, stands desiring to embrace thee. Hasten therefore to do him reverence. [Sacontalá *modestly bows to him.*

Can. Mayst thou be cherished by thy husband, as Sarmishthà was cherished by Yayáti! Mayst thou bring forth a sovereign of the world, as she brought forth Puru!

Gaut. This, my child, is not a mere benediction; it is a boon actually conferred.

Can. My best beloved, come and walk with me round the sacrificial fire.—[*They all advanced.*]—May these fires preserve thee! Fires which spring to their appointed stations on the holy hearth, and consume the consecrated wood, while the fresh blades of mysterious Cusa lie scattered around them! Sacramental fires, which destroy sin with the rising fumes of clarified butter!—[Sacontalá *walks with solemnity round the hearth.*]—Now set out, my darling, on thy auspicious journey.—[*Looking round.*]—Where are the attendants, the two Misras?

Enter Sárngarava *and* Sáradwata.

Both. Holy sage, we are here.

Can. My son, Sárngarava, show thy sister her way.

Sárn. Come, damsel.——— [*They all advance.*

Can. Hear, all ye trees of this hallow forest; ye trees, in which the sylvan goddesses have their abode; hear, and proclaim, that Sacontalá is going to the palace of her wedded lord; she who drank not, though thirsty, before you were watered; she who cropped not, through affection for you, one of your fresh leaves, though she would have been pleased with such an ornament for her locks; she whose chief delight was in the season when your branches are spangled with flowers!

CHORUS *of invisible* WOODNYMPHS.

May her way be attended with prosperity! May propitious breezes sprinkle, for her delight, the odoriferous dust of rich blossoms! May pools of clear water, green with the leaves of the lotos, refresh her as she walks! and may shady branches be her defence from the scorching sun-beams!

[*All listen with admiration.*

Sárn. Was that the voice of the Cócila wishing a happy journey to Sacontalá?—Or did the nymphs, who are allied to the pious inhabitants of these woods, repeat the warbling of the musical bird, and make its greeting their own?

Gaut. Daughter, the sylvan goddesses, who love their kindred hermits, have wished you prosperity, and are entitled to humble thanks.

[Sacontalá *walks round, bowing to the nymphs.*

Sac. [*Aside to* Priyamvadá.] Delighted as I am, O Priyamvadá with the thought of seeing again the son of my lord, yet, on leaving this grove, my early asylum, I am scarce able to walk.

Pri. You lament not alone.——Mark the affliction of the forest itself when the time of your departure approaches!——The female antelope browses no more on the collected Cusa grass; and the peahen ceases to dance on the lawn: the very plants of the grove, whose pale leaves fall on the ground, lose their strength and their beauty.

Sac. Venerable father, suffer me to address this Mádhaví creeper, whose red blossoms inflame the grove.

Can. My child, I know thy affection for it.

Sac. [*Embracing the plant.*] O most radiant of twining plants, receive my embraces, and return them with thy flexible arms: from this day, though removed to a fatal distance, I shall for ever be thine.—O beloved father, consider this creeper as myself.

Can. My darling, thy amiable qualities have gained thee a husband equal to thyself: such an event has been long, for thy sake, the chief object of my heart; and now, since my solicitude for thy marriage is at an end, I will marry thy favorite plant to the bridegroom Amra, who sheds fragrance near her.——Proceed, my child, on thy journey.

Sac. [*Approaching the two damsels.*] Sweet friends, let this Mádhaví creeper be a precious deposit in your hands.

Anu. and Pri. Alas! in whose care shall we be left?

[*They both weep.*

Can. Tears are vain, Anusúyá: our Sacontalá ought rather to be supported by your firmness, than weakened by your weeping. [*All advance.*

Sac. Father! when yon female antelope, who now moves slowly from the weight of the young ones with which she is pregnant, shall be delivered of them, send me, I beg, a kind message with tidings of her safety.——Do not forget.

Can. My beloved, I will not forget it.

Sac. [*Advancing, then stopping.*] Ah! what is it that clings to the skirts of my robe, and detains me?

[*She turns round, and looks.*

Can. It is thy adopted child, the little fawn, whose mouth, when the sharp points of Cusa grass had wounded it, has been so often smeared by thy hand with the healing oil of Ingudí; who has been so often fed by thee with a handful of Syámáka grains, and now will not leave the footstep of his protectress.

Sac. Why dost thou weep, tender fawn, for me, who

must leave our common dwelling-place ?—As thou wast reared by me when thou hadst lost thy mother, who died soon after thy birth, so will my foster-father attend thee, when we are separated, with anxious care.—Return, poor thing, return.—we must part. [*She bursts into tears.*

Can. Thy tears, my child, ill suit the occasion : we shall all meet again : be firm : see the direct road before thee, and follow it.—When the big tear lurks beneath thy beautiful eyelashes, let thy resolution check its first efforts to disengage itself.—In thy passage over this earth, where the paths are now high, now low, and the true path seldom distinguished, the traces of thy feet must needs be unequal; but virtue will press thee right onward.

Sárn. It is a sacred rule, holy sage, that a benevolent man should accompany a traveller till he meet with abundance of water ; and that rule you have carefully observed : we are now near the brink of a large pool. Give us, therefore, your commands, and return.

Can. Let us rest a while under the shade of this Vata tree——[*They all go to the shade.*]—What message can I send with propriety to the noble Dushmanta? [*He meditates.*

Anu. [*Aside to* Sacontalá.] My beloved friend, every heart in our asylum is fixed on you alone, and all are afflicted by your departure.—Look ; the bird Chacraváca, called by his mate, who is almost hidden by water lilies, gives her no answer ; but having dropped from his bill the fibres of lotos stalks which he had plucked, gazes on you with inexpressible tenderness.

Can. My son Sárngarava, remember, when thou shalt present Sacontalá to the king, to address him thus, in my name : "Considering us hermits as virtuous, indeed, but rich only in devotion, and considering also thy own exalted birth, retain thy love for this girl, which arose in thy bosom without any interference of' her kindred ; and look on her among thy wives with the same kindness which they experience ; more than that cannot be demanded ; since particular affection must depend on the will of heaven."

Sárn. Your message, venerable man, is deeply rooted in my remembrance.

Can. [*Looking tenderly at* Sacontalá.] Now, my darling, thou too must be gently admonished.—We, who are humble foresters, are yet acquainted with the world which we have forsaken.

Sárn. Nothing can be unknown to the wise.

Can. Hear, my daughter——When thou art settled in the mansion of thy husband, show due reverence to him and to those whom he reveres : though he have other wives, be rather an affectionate handmaid to them than a rival.—Should he displease thee, let not thy resentment lead thee to disobedience.——In thy conduct to thy domestics be rigidly just and impartial; and seek not eagerly thy own gratifications.——By such behaviour young women become respectable; but perverse wives are the bane of a family.——What thinks Gautamí of this lesson ?

Gaut. It is incomparable :——my child, be sure to remember it.

Can. Come, my beloved girl, give a parting embrace to me and to thy tender companions.

Sac. Must Anusúyá and Priyamvadá return to the hermitage ?

Can. They too, my child, must be suitably married; and it would not be proper for them yet to visit the city; but Gautamí will accompany thee.

Sac. [*Embracing him.*] Removed from the bosom of my father, like a young sandal tree, rent from the hills of Malaya, how shall I exist in a strange soil ?

Can. Be not so anxious. When thou shalt be mistress of a family, and comfort of a king, thou mayst, indeed, be occasionally perplexed by the intricate affairs which arise from exuberance of wealth, but wilt then think lightly of this transient affliction, especially when thou shalt have a son (and a son thou wilt have) bright as the rising day-star.——Know also with certainty, that the body must necessarily, at the appointed moment, be separated from the soul : who, then, can be immoderately afflicted, when the weaker bounds of extrinsic relations are loosened, or even broken.

Sac. [*Falling at his feet.*] My father, I thus humbly declare my veneration for you.

Can. Excellent girl, may my effort for thy happiness prove successful.

Sac. [*Approaching her two companions.*] Come, then, my beloved friends, embrace me together. [*They embrace her.*

Anu. My friend, if the virtuous monarch should not at once recollect you, only show him the ring on which his own name is engraved.

Sac. [*Starting.*] My heart flutters at the bare apprehension which you have raised.

Pri. Fear not, sweet Sacontalá: love always raises ideas of misery, which are seldom or never realised.

Sárn. Holy sage, the sun has risen to a considerable height: let the queen hasten her departure.

Sac. [*Again embracing* Canna.] When, my father, oh! when again shall I behold this asylum of virtue?

Can. Daughter, when thou shalt long have been wedded, like this fruitful earth, to the pious monarch, and shalt have borne him a son, whose car shall be matchless in battle, thy lord shall transfer to him the burden of empire, and thou, with thy Dushmanta, shalt again seek tranquillity, before thy final departure, in this loved and consecrated grove.

Gaut. My child, the proper time for our journey passes away rapidly: suffer thy father to return.——Go, venerable man, go back to thy mansion, from which she is doomed to be so long absent.

Can. Sweet child, this delay interrupts my religious duties.

Sac. You, my father, will perform them long without sorrow; but I, alas! am destined to bear affliction.

Can. O! my daughter, compel me not to neglect my daily devotions.——[*Sighing.*]—No, my sorrow will not be diminished.—Can it cease, my beloved, when the plants which rise luxuriantly from the hallowed grains which thy hand has strown before my cottage, are continually in my sight?—Go, may thy journey prosper.

[Sacontalá *goes out with* Gautamí *and the two Misras.*

Both damsels. [*Looking after* Sacontalá *with anguish.*] Alas! alas! our beloved is hidden by the thick trees.

Can. My children, since your friend is at length departed, check your immoderate grief, and follow me. [*They all turn back.*

Both. Holy father, the grove will be a perfect vacuity without Sacontalá.

Can. Your affection will certainly give it that appearance. ——[*He walks round, meditating.*]—Ah me!—Yes; at last my weak mind has attained its due firmness after the departure of my Sacontalá.—In truth a daughter must sooner or later be the property of another; and, having now sent her to her lord, I find my soul clear and undisturbed, like that of a man who has restored to its owner an inestimable deposit which he long had kept with solicitude. [*They go out*

ACT V.

SCENE—*The* PALACE.

An old Chamberlain, *sighing.*

Chamberlain.

ALAS! what a decrepit old age have I attained!——This wand, which I first held for the discharge of my customary duties in the secret apartments of my prince, is now my support, whilst I walk feebly through the multitude of years which I have passed.——I must now mention to the king, as he goes through the palace, an event which concerns himself: it must not be delayed.—[*Advancing slowly.*]—What is it?—Oh! I recollect: the devout pupils of Canna desire an audience.—How strange a thing is human life!—The intellects of an old man seem at one time luminous, and then on a sudden are involved in darkness, like the flame of a lamp at the point of extinction.——*He walks round and looks.*]—There is Dushmanta: he has been attending to his people, as to his own family; and now with a tranquil heart seeks a solitary chamber; as an elephant the chief of his herd, having grazed the whole morning, and being heated by the meridian sun, repairs to a cool station during the oppressive heats.——Since the king is just risen from his tribunal, and must be fatigued, I am almost afraid to inform him at present that Canna's pupils are arrived: yet how should they who support nations enjoy rest?—The sun yokes his bright steeds for the labor of many hours; the gale breathes by night and by day; the prince of serpents continually sustains the weight of this earth; and equally incessant is the toil of that man, whose revenue arises from a sixth part of his people's income.

[*He walks about.*

Enter Dushmanta, Mádhavya, *and attendants.*

Dushm. [*Looking oppressed with business.*] Every petitioner having attained justice, is departed happy; but kings who perform their duties conscientiously are afflicted without end.—The anxiety of acquiring dominion gives extreme pain; and when it is firmly established, the cares of supporting the nation incessantly harass the sovereign; as a large umbrella, of which a man carries the staff in his own hand, fatigues while it shades him.

Behind the scenes. May the king be victorious.!

Two Bards *repeat stanzas.*

First Bard. Thou seekest not thy own pleasure: no; it is for the people that thou art harassed from day to day. Such, when thou wast created, was the disposition implanted in thy soul! Thus a branchy tree bears on his head the scorching sunbeams, while his broad shade allays the fever of those who seek shelter under him.

Second Bard. When thou wieldest the rod of justice, thou bringest to order all those who have deviated from the path of virtue: thou biddest contention cease: thou wast formed for the preservation of thy people: thy kindred possess, indeed, considerable wealth; but so boundless is thy affection, that all thy subjects are considered by thee as thy kinsmen.

Dushm. [*Listening.*] That sweet poetry refreshes me after the toil of giving judgments and public orders.

Mádh. Yes; as a tired bull is refreshed when the people say, "There goes the lord of cattle."

Dushm. [*Smiling.*] Oh! art thou here, my friend: let us take our seats together. [*The king and* Mádhavya *sit down.*—*Music behind the scenes.*

Mádh. Listen, my royal friend. I hear a well-tuned Víná sounding, as if it were in concert with the lutes of the gods, from yonder apartment.—The queen Hansamatì is preparing, I imagine. to greet you with a new song.

Dushm. Be silent, that I may listen.

Cham. [*Aside.*] The king's mind seems intent on some other business. I must wait his leisure. [*Retiring on one side.*

SONG. [*Behind the scenes.*]

"Sweet bee, who, desirous of extracting fresh honey, wast

wont to kiss the soft border of the new-blown Amra flower, how canst thou now be satisfied with the water lily, and forget the first object of thy love ?"

Dushm. The ditty breathes a tender passion.

Mádh. Does the king know its meaning ? It is too deep for me.

Dushm. [*Smiling.*] I was once in love with Hansamatí, and am now reproved for continuing so long absent from her.—Friend Mádhavya, inform the queen in my name that I feel the reproof.

Mádh. As the king commands ; but—[*Rising slowly.*]—My friend, you are going to seize a sharp lance with another man's hand. I cannot relish your commission to an enraged woman.—A hermit cannot be happy till he has taken leave of all passion whatever.

Dushm. Go, my kind friend : the urbanity of thy discourse will appease her.

Mádh. What an errand ! [*He goes out.*

Dushm. [*Aside.*] Ah ! What makes me so melancholy on hearing a mere song on absence, when I am not in fact separated from any real object of my affection ?—Perhaps the sadness of men, otherwise happy, on seeing beautiful forms and listening to sweet melody, arises from some faint remembrance of past joys and the traces of connections in a former state of existence.

[*He sits pensive and sorrowful.*

Cham. [*Advancing humbly.*] May our sovereign be victorious !—Two religious men, with some women, are come from their abode in a forest near the Snowy Mountains, and bring a message from Canna.—The king will command.

Dushm. [*Surprised.*] What ! are pious hermits arrived in the company of women ?

Cham. It is even so.

Dushm. Order the priest Sómaratá, in my name, to shew them due reverence in the form appointed by the Véda ; and bid him attend me. I shall wait for my holy guests in a place fit for their reception.

Cham. I obey. [*He goes out.*

Dushm. Warder, point the way to the hearth of the consecrated fire.

Ward. This, O king, this is the way.—[*He walks before.*]—Here is the entrance of the hallowed enclosure; and there stands the venerable cow to be milked for the sacrifice, looking bright from the recent sprinkling of mystic water.—Let the king ascend. [Dushmanta *is raised to the place of sacrifice on the shoulders of his Warders.*

Dushm. What message can the pious Canna have sent me?—Has the devotion of his pupils been impeded by evil spirits—or by what other calamity?—Or has any harm, alas! befallen the poor herds who graze in the hallowed forest?—Or have the sins of the king tainted the flowers and fruits of the creepers planted by female hermits?—My mind is entangled in a labyrinth of confused apprehensions.

Ward. What our sovereign imagines, cannot possibly have happened; since the hermitage has been rendered secure from evil by the mere sound of his bowstring. The pious men, whom the king's benevolence has made happy, are come, I presume, to do him homage.

Enter. Sárngarava, Sáradwata *and* Gautamí, *leading* Sacontalá *by the hand; and before them the old* Chamberlain *and the* Priest.

Cham. This way, respectable strangers; come this way.

Sárn. My friend Sáradwata, there sits the king of men, who has felicity at command, yet shows equal respect to all: here no subject, even of the lowest class, is received with contempt. Nevertheless, my soul having ever been free from attachment to worldly things, I consider this hearth, although a crowd now surround it, as the station merely of consecrated fire.

Sárad. I was not less confounded than yourself on entering the populous city; but now I look on it, as a man just bathed in pure water, on a man smeared with oil and dust, as the pure on the impure, as the waking on the sleeping, as the free man on the captive, as the independent on the slave.

Priest. Thence it is, that men, like you two, are so elevated above other mortals.

Sac. [*Perceiving a bad omen.*] Venerable mother, I feel my right eye throb ! What means this involuntary motion ?

Gaut. Heaven avert the omen, my sweet child ! May every delight attend thee ! [*They all advance.*

Priest. [*Shewing the king to them.*] There, holy men is the protector of the people ; who has taken his seat, and expects you.

Sárn. This is what we wished ; yet we have no private interest in the business. It is ever thus : trees are bent by the abundance of their fruit ; clouds are brought low, when they teem with salubrious rain ; and the real benefactors of mankind are not elated by riches.

Ward. O king, the holy guests appear before you with placid looks, indicating their affection.

Dushm. [*Gazing at* Sacontalá.] Ah ! what damsel is that, whose mantle conceals the far greater part of her beautiful form ?—She looks, among the hermits, like a fresh green bud among faded and yellow leaves.

Ward. This at least, O king, is apparent ; that she has a form which deserves to be seen more distinctly.

Dushm. Let her still be covered : she seems pregnant ; and the wife of another must not be seen even by me.

Sac. [*Aside, with her hand to her bosom.*] O my heart, why dost thou palpitate ?—Remember the beginning of thy lord's affection, and be tranquil.

Priest. May the king prosper ! The respectable guests have been honored as the law ordains ; and they have now a message to deliver from their spiritual guide ; let the king deign to hear it.

Dushm. [*With reverence.*] I am attentive.

Both Misras. [*Extending their hands.*] Victory attend thy banners !

Dushm. I respectfully greet you both.

Both. Blessings on our sovereign !

Dushm. Has your devotion been uninterrupted ?

Sárn. How should our rites be disturbed, when thou art

the preserver of all creatures? How, when the bright sun blazes, should darkness cover the world?

Dushm. [*Aside.*] The name of royalty produces, I suppose, all worldly advantages!—[*Aloud.*] Does the holy Canna then prosper?

Sárn. O king, they who gather the fruits of devotion may command prosperity. He first inquires affectionately whether thy arms are successful, and then addresses thee in these words:—

Dushm. What are his orders?

Sárn. "The contract of marriage, reciprocally made between thee and this girl, my daughter, I confirm with tender regard; since thou art celebrated as the most honorable of men and my Sacontalá is Virtue herself in a human form, no blasphemous complaint will henceforth be made against Brahmá for suffering discordant matches: he has now united a bride and bridegroom with qualities equally transcendent.—Since, therefore, she is pregnant by thee, receive her in thy palace, that she may perform, in conjunction with thee, the duties prescribed by religion."

Gaut. Great king, thou hast a mild aspect; and I wish to address thee in few words.

Dushm. [*Smiling.*] Speak, venerable matron.

Gaut. She waited not the return of her spiritual father; nor were thy kindred consulted by thee. You two only were present, when your nuptials were solemnized: now, therefore converse freely together in the absence of all others.

Sac. [*Aside.*] What will my lord say?

Dushm. [*Aside, perplexed.*] How strange an adventure!

Sac. [*Aside.*] Ah me! how disdainfully he seems to receive the message!

Sárn. [*Aside.*] What means that phrase which I overheard, "How strange an adventure?"—[*Aloud.*]—Monarch, thou knowest the hearts of men. Let a wife behave ever so discreetly, the world will think ill of her, if she live only with her paternal kinsmen; and a lawful wife now requests, as her kindred also humbly entreat, that whether she be loved or not, she may pass her days in the mansion of her husband.

Dushm. What sayest thou ! Am I the lady's husband ?

Sac. [*Aside, with anguish.*] O my heart, thy fears have proved just.

Sárn. Does it become a magnificent prince to depart from the rules of religion and honor, merely because he repents of his engagements ?

Dushm. With what hope of success could this groundless fable have been invented ?

Sárn. [*Angrily.*] The minds of those whom power intoxicates are perpetually changing.

Dushm. I am reproved with too great severity.

Gaut. [*To* Sacontalá.] Be not ashamed, my sweet child : let me take off thy mantle, that the king may recollect thee.

[*She unveils her.*

Dushm. [*Aside, looking at* Sacontalá.] While I am doubtful whether this unblemished beauty which is displayed before me has not been possessed by another, I resemble a bee fluttering at the close of night over a blossom filled with dew ; and in this state of mind, I neither can enjoy nor forsake her.

Ward. [*Aside to* Dushmanta.] The king best knows his rights and his duties : but who would hesitate when a woman, bright as a gem, brings lustre to the apartments of his palace ?

Sárn. What, O king, does thy strange silence import ?

Dushm. Holy man, I have been meditating again and again, but have no recollection of my marriage with this lady. How then can I lay aside all consideration of my military tribe, and admit into my palace a young woman who is pregnant by another husband ?

Sac. [*Aside.*] Ah ! wo is me.—Can there be a doubt even of our nuptials ?—The tree of my hope, which had risen so luxuriantly, is at once broken down.

Sárn. Beware, lest the godlike sage, who would have bestowed on thee, as a free gift, his inestimable treasure, which thou hadst taken, like a base robber, should now cease to think of thee, who art lawfully married to his daughter, and should confine all his thoughts to her whom thy perfidy disgraces.

Sárad. Rest a while, my Sárngarava; and thou, Sacontalá, take thy turn to speak; since thy lord has declared his forgetfulness.

Sac. [*Aside.*] If his affection has ceased, of what use will it be to recall his remembrance of me?—Yet, if my soul must endure torment, be it so: I will speak to him.——[*Aloud to* Dushmanta.]—O my husband!——[*Pausing.*]—Or (if the just application of that sacred word be still doubted by thee) O son of Puru, is it becoming, that, having been once enamoured of me in the consecrated forest, and having shown the excess of thy passion, thou shouldst this day deny me with bitter expressions?

Dushm. [*Covering his ears.*] Be the crime removed from my soul!—Thou hast been instructed for some base purpose to vilify me, and make me fall from the dignity which I have hitherto supported; as a river which has burst its banks and altered its placid current, overthrows the trees that had risen aloft on them.

Sac. If thou sayst this merely from want of recollection, I will restore thy memory by producing thy own ring, with thy name engraved on it!

Dushm. A capital invention!

Sac. [*Looking at her finger.*] Ah me! I have no ring.

[*She fixes her eyes, with anguish on* Gautamí.]

Gaut. The fatal ring must have dropped, my child from thy hand, when thou tookest up water to pour on thy head in the pool of Sachítírt'hr, near the station of Sacrávatára.

Dushm. [*Smiling.*] So skilful are women in finding ready excuses!

Sac. The power of Bramá must prevail: I will yet mention one circumstance.

Dushm. I must submit to hear the tale.

Sac. One day, in a grove of Vétasas, thou tookest water in thy hand from its natural vase of lotos leaves——

Dushm. What followed?

Sac. At that instant a little fawn, which I had reared as my own child, approached thee; and thou saydst with benevolence: "Drink thou first, gentle fawn." He would not drink from the hand of a stranger, but received water eagerly from mine; when thou saidst, with increasing affection: "Thus every creature loves its companions; you are both foresters alike, and both alike, amiable."

Dushm. By such interested and honied falsehoods are the souls of voluptuaries ensnared!

Gaut. Forbear, illustrious prince, to speak harshly. She was bred in a sacred grove where she learned no guile.

Dushm. Pious matron, the dexterity of females, even when they are untaught, appears in those of a species different from our own.—What would it be if they were duly instructed! —The female Cócilas, before they fly towards the firmament, leave their eggs to be hatched, and their young fed, by birds who have no relation to them.

Sac. [*With anger.*] Oh! void of honor, thou measurest all the world by thy own bad heart. What prince ever resembled, or ever will resemble, thee, who wearest the garb of religion and virtue, but in truth art a base deceiver; like a deep well whose mouth is covered with smiling plants!

Dushm. [*Aside.*] The rusticity of her education makes her speak thus angrily and inconcistently with female decorum. —She looks indignant; her eye glows; and her speech, formed of harsh terms, faulters as she utters them. Her lip, ruddy as the Bimba fruit, quivers as if it were nipped with frost; and her eyebrows, naturally smooth and equal, are at once irregularly contracted.—Thus having failed in circumventing me by the apparent lustre of simplicity, she has recourse to wrath, and snaps in two the bow of Cáma, which, if she had not belonged to another, might have wounded me.—[*Aloud.*]—The heart of Dushmanta, young woman, is known to all; and thine is betrayed by thy present demeanor.

Sac. [*Ironically.*] You kings are in all cases to be credited implicitly: you perfectly know the respect which is due to virtue and to mankind; while females, however modest, however virtuous, know nothing, and speak nothing truly.—In a happy hour I came hither to seek the object of my affection: in a happy moment I received the hand of a prince descended from Puru; a prince who had won my confidence by the honey of his words, whilst his heart concealed the weapon that was to pierce mine. [*She hides her face and weeps.*

Sárn. This insufferable mutability of the king's temper kindles my wrath.—Henceforth let all be circumspect before they form secret connections: a friendship hastily contracted, when both hearts are not perfectly known, must ere long become enmity.

Dushm. Wouldst thou force me then to commit an enormous crime, relying solely on her smooth speeches?

Sárn. [*Scornfully.*] Thou hast heard an answer.—The words of an incomparable girl, who never learned what iniquity was, are here to receive no credit; while they, whose learning consists in accusing others, and inquiring into crimes, are the only persons who speak truth?

Dushm. O man of unimpeached veracity, I certainly am what thou describest; but what would be gained by accusing thy female associate?

Sárn. Eternal misery.

Dushm. No; misery will never be the portion of Puru's defcendants.

Sárn. What avils our altercation?—O king, we have obeyed the commands of our preceptor, and now return. Sacontalà is by law thy wife, whether thou desert or acknowledge her; and the dominion of a husband is absolute.—Go before us, Gautamí. [*The two Misras and* Gautamí *returning.*

Sac. I have been deceived by this perfidious man; but will you, my friends, will you also forsake me? [*Following them.*

Gaut. [*Looking back.*] My son, Sacontalá follows us with affectionate supplications. What can she do here with a faithless husband; she who is all tenderness?

Sárn. [*Angrily to* Sacontalá.] O wife, who seest the faults of thy lord, dost thou desire independence?

[Sacontalá *stops, and trembles.*

Sárad. Let the queen hear. If thou beest what the king proclaims thee, what right hast thou to complain? But if thou knowest the purity of thy own soul, it will become thee to wait as a handmaid in the mansion of thy lord. Stay, then, where thou art: we must return to Carma.

Dushm. Deceive her not, holy men, with vain expectations. The moon opens the night flower; and the sun makes the water lily blossom: each is confined to its own object: and thus a virtuous man abstains from any connection with the wife of another.

Sárn. Yet thou, O king, who fearest to offend religion and virtue, art not afraid to desert thy wedded wife; pretending that the variety of thy public affairs has made thee forget thy private contract.

Dushm. [*To his Priest.*] I really have no remembrance of any such engagement; and I ask thee, my spritual counsellor, whether of the two offences be the greater, to forsake my own wife, or to have an intercourse with the wife of another?

Priest. [*After some deliberation.*] We may adopt an expedient between both.

Dushm. Let my venerable guide command.

Priest. The young woman may dwell till her dilivery in my house.

Dushm. For what purpose?

Priest. Wise astrologers have assured the king, that he will be the father of an illustrious prince, whose dominion will be bounded by the western and eastern seas: now, if the holy man's daughter shall bring forth a son whose hands and feet bear the marks of extensive sovereignty, I will do homage to her as my queen, and conduct her to the royal apartments; if not, she shall return in due time to her father.

Dushm. Be it as you judge proper.

Priest. [To Sacontalá.] This way, my daughter, follow me.

Sac. O earth! mild goddess, give me a place within thy bosom!

[*She goes out weeping with the Priest; while the two Misras go out by a different way with* Gautamí——Dushmanta *stands meditating on the beauty of* Sacontalá; *but the imprecation still clouds his memory.*]

Behind the scenes. Oh! miraculous event!

Dushm. [*Listening.*] What can have happened!

The Priest *re-enters.*

Priest. Hear, O king, the stupendous event. When Canna's pupils had departed, Sacontalá, bewailing her adverse fortune, extended her arms and wept; when——

Dushm. What then?

Priest. A body of light, in a female shape, descended near Apsarastírt'ha, where the nymphs of heaven are worshiped; and having caught her hastily in her bosom, disappeared.

[*All express astonishment.*

Dushm. I suspected from the beginning some work of sorcery.—The business is over; and it is needless to reason more on it.—Let thy mind, Sómaráta, be at rest.

Priest. May the king be victorious. [*He goes out.*

Dushm. Chamberlain, I have been greatly harassed; and thou, Warder, go before me to a place of repose.

Ward. This way; let the king come this way.

Dushm. [*Advancing, aside.*] I cannot with all my efforts recollect my nuptials with the daughter of the hermit; yet so agitated is my heart, that it almost induces me to believe her story. [*All go out.*

ACT VI.

SCENE—A Street.

Enter a Superintendent of Police with two Officers, leading a man with his hands bound.

First Officer. Striking the prisoner.

TAKE that, Cumbhílaca if Cumbhílaca be thy name; and tell us now where thou gottest this ring, bright with a large gem, on which the king's name is engraved.

Cumbh. [*Trembling.*] Spare me, I entreat your honors to spare me: I am not guilty of so great a crime as you suspect.

First Off. O distinguished Bráhmen, didst thou then receive it from the king as a reward of some important service?

Cumbh. Only hear me; I am a poor fisherman dwelling at Sacrávatára——

Second Off. Did we ask, thou thief, about thy tribe or thy dwelling place.

Sup. O Súchaca, let the fellow tell his own story.——Now conceal nothing, sirrah.

First Off. Dost thou hear? Do as our master commands.

Cumbh. I am a man who support my family by catching fish in nets, or with hooks, and by various other contrivances.

Sup. [*Laughing.*] A virtuous way of gaining a livelihood!

Cumbh. Blame me not, master. The occupation of our forefathers, how low soever, must not be forsaken; and a man who kills animals for sale may have a tender heart though his act be cruel.

Sup. Go on, go on.

Cumbh. One day having caught a large Róhita fish, I cut it open, and saw this bright ring in its stomach; but when I offered to sell it, I was apprehended by your honors. So far only am I guilty of taking the ring. Will you now continue beating and bruising me to death?

Sup. [*Smelling the ring.*] It is certain, Jáluca, that this gem has been in the body of a fish, The case requires consideration; and I will mention it to some of the king's household.

Both Off. Come on, cutpurse. [*They advance.*

Sup. Stand here, Súchaca, at the great gate of the city, and wait for me, while I speak to some of the officers in the palace.

Both Off. Go, Rájayucta. May the king favor thee.

[*The Superintendent goes out.*

Second Off. Our master will stay, I fear, a long while.

First Off. Yes; access to kings can only be had at their leisure.

Second Off. The tips of my fingers itch, my friend Jáluca, to kill this cutpurse.

Cumbh. You would put to death an innocent man.

First Off. [*Looking.*] Here comes our master.—The king has decided quickly. Now, Cumbhílaca, you will either see your compainions again, or be the food of shakàls and vultures.

The Superintendent re-enters.

Sup. Let the fisherman immediately——

Cumbh. [*In an agony.*] Oh! I am a dead man.

Sup.——be discharged.—Hola! set him at liberty. The king says he knows his innocence; and his story is true.

Second Off. As our master commands.——The fellow is brought back from the mansion of Yama, to which he was hastening. [*Unbinding the fisherman.*

Cumbh. [*Bowing.*] My lord, I owe my life to your kindness.

Sup. Rise, friend; and hear with delight that the king gives thee a sum of money equal to the full value of the ring: it is a fortune to a man in thy station. [*Giving him the money.*

Cumbh. [*With rapture.*] I am transported with joy.

First Off. This vagabond seems to be taken down from the stake, and set on the back of a state elephant.

Second Off. The king, I suppose, has a great affection for his gem.

Sup. Not for its intrinsic value; but I guessed the cause of his ecstasy when he saw it.

Both Off. What could occasion it?

Sup. I suspect that it called to his memory some person who has a place in his heart; for though his mind be naturally firm, yet, from the moment when he beheld the ring, he was for some minutes excessively agitated.

Second Off. Our master has given the king extreme pleasure.

First Off. Yes; and by the means of this fish-catcher. [*Looking fiercely at him.*

Cumbh. Be not angry—Half the money shall be divided between you to purchase wine.

First Off. Oh! now thou art our beloved friend.—Good wine is the first object of our affection.—Let us go together to the vintners. [*They all go out.*

SCENE—*The* GARDEN *of the* PALACE.

The Nymph Misracésí *appears in the air.*

Misr. My first task was duly performed when I went to bathe in the Nymphs' pool; and I now must see with my own eyes how the virtuous king is afflicted.——Sacontalá is dear to this heart, because she is the daughter of my beloved Ménacà, from whom I received both commissions.—[*She looks round.*]—Ah! on a day full of delights the monarch's family seem oppressed with some new sorrow.——By exerting my supernatural power I could know what has passed; but respect must be shown to the desire of Ménacà.—I will retire, therefore, among those plants, observe what is done without being visible.

[*She descends and takes her station.*

Enter two Damsels, attendants on the God of Love.

First Dams. [*Looking at an Amra flower.*] The blossoms of yon Amra, waving on the green stalk, are fresh and light as the breath of this vernal month. I must present the goddess Retí with a basket of them.

Second Dams. Why, my Parabhriticá, dost thou mean to present it alone?

First Dams. O my friend Madhucaricá, when a female Cócilà, which my name implies, sees a blooming Amra, she becomes entranced, and loses her recollection.

Second Dams. [*With transport.*] What! is the season of sweets actually returned?

First Dams. Yes; the season in which we must sing of nothing but wine and love.

Second Dams. Support me, then, while I climb up this tree, and strip it of its fragrant gems, which we will carry as an offering to Cáma.

First Dams. If I assist, I must have a moiety of the reward which the god will bestow.

Second Dams. To be sure, and without any previous bargain. We are only one soul, you know, though Brahmà has given it two bodies.——[*She climbs up, and gathers the flowers.*] —Ah! the buds are hardly opened.——Here is one a little expanded, which diffuses a charming odour——[*Taking a handful of buds.*]—This flower is sacred to the god who bears a fish on his banner.—O sweet blossom, which I now consecrate, thou well deservest to point the sixth arrow of Cámadéva, who now takes his bow to pierce myriads of youthful hearts.

[*She throws down a blossom.*

The old Chamberlain *enters.*

Cham. [*Angrily.*] Desist from breaking off those half-opened buds: there will be no jubilee this year; our king has forbidden it.

Both Dams. Oh! pardon us. We really knew not the prohibition.

Cham. You knew it not!—Even the trees which the spring was decking, and the birds who perch on them, sympathize with our monarch. Thence it is, that yon buds, which have long appeared, shed not yet their prolific dust; and the flower of the Curuvaca, though perfectly formed, remains veiled in a closed chalice; while the voice of the Cócilà, though the cold dews fall no more, is fixed within his throat; and even Smara, the god of desire, replaces the shaft half-drawn from his quiver.

Misr. [*Aside.*] The king, no doubt, is constant and tender-hearted.

First Dams. A few days ago, Mitravasu, the governor of our province, dispatched us to kiss the feet of the king, and we come to decorate his groves and gardens with various emblems: thence it is, that we heard nothing of his interdict.

Cham. Beware then of reiterating your offence.

Second Dams. To obey our lord will certainly be our delight; but, if we are permitted to hear the story, tell us, we pray, what has induced our sovereign to forbid the usual festivity.

Misr. [*Aside.*] Kings are generally fond of gay entertainments; and there must be some weighty reason for the prohibition.

Cham. [*Aside.*] The affair is public: why should I not satisfy them?——[*Aloud.*]—Has not the calamitous desertion of Sacontalà reached your ears?

First. Dams. We heard her tale from the governer, as far as the sight of the fatal ring.

Cham. Then I have little to add.——When the king's memory was restored, by the sight of his gem, he instantly exclamed: "Yes, the incomparable Sacontalá is my lawful wife; and when I rejected her, I had lost my reason."—He showed strong marks of extreme affliction and penitence; and from that moment he has abhorred the pleasures of life. No longer does he exert his respectable talents from day to day for the good of his people: he prolongs his nights without closing his eyes, perpetually rolling on the edge of his couch; and he rises, he pronounces not one sentence aptly; mistaking the names of the women in his apartments, and through distraction, calling each of them Sacontalá: then he sits abashed, with his head long bent on his knees.

Misr. [*Aside.*] This is pleasing to me, very pleasing.

Cham. By reason of the deep sorrow which now prevails in his heart, the vernal jubilee has been interdicted.

Both Dams. The prohibition is highly proper.

Behind the scenes. Make way! The king is passing.

Cham. [*Listening.*] Here comes the monarch: depart therefore, damsels, to your own provinces. [*The two Damsels go out.*

Dushmanta *enters in penitential weeds, preceded by a Warder, and attended by* Mádhavya.

Cham. [*Looking at the king.*] Ah! how majestic are noble forms in every habiliment!—Our prince, even in the garb of affliction, is a venerable object.—Though he has abandoned pleasure, ornaments, and business; though he is become so thin, that his golden bracelet falls loosened even down to his wrist; though his lips are parched with the heat of his sighs, and his eyes are fixed open by long sorrow and want of sleep, yet am I dazzled by the blaze of virtue which beams in his countenance like a diamond exquisitely polished.

Misr. [*Aside, gazing on* Dushmanta.] With good reason is my beloved Sacontalá, though disgraced and rejected, heavily oppressed with grief through the absence of this youth.

Dushm. [*Advancing slowly, in deep meditation.*] When my darling with an antelope's eyes would have reminded me of our love, I was assuredly slumbering; but excess of misery has awakened me.

Misr. [*Aside.*] The charming girl will at last be happy.

Mádh. [*Aside.*] This monarch of ours is caught again in the gale of affection; and I hardly know a remedy for his illness.

Cham. [*Approaching* Dushmanta.] May the king be victorious!—Let him survey yon fine woodland, these cool walks, and this blooming garden; where he may repose with pleasure on banks of delight.

Dushm. [*Not attending to him*]. Warder, inform the chief minister in my name, that having resolved on a long absence from the city, I do not mean to sit for some time in the tribunal; but let him write and dispatch to me all the cases that may arise among my subjects.

Ward. As the king commands. [*He goes out.*

Dushm. [*To the* Chamberlain.] And thou, Párvatáyana, neglect not thy stated business.

Cham. By no means. [*He goes out.*

Mádh. You have not left a fly in the garden.—Amuse yourself now in this retreat, which seems pleased with the departure of the dewy season.

Dushm. O Mádhavya, when persons accused of great offences prove wholly innocent, see how their accusers are punished !——A phrensy obstructed my remembrance of any former love for the daughter of the sage; and now the heart-born god, who delights in giving pain, has fixed in his bow-string a new shaft pointed with the blossom of an Amra.——The fatal ring having restored my memory, see me deplore with tears of repentance the loss of my best beloved, whom I rejected without cause ; see me overwhelmed with sorrow, even while the return of spring fills the hearts of all others with pleasure.

Ma'dh. Be still, my friend, whilst I break Love's arrows with my staff. [*He strikes off some flowers from an Amra tree.*

Dushm. [*Meditating.*] Yes, I acknowledge the supreme power of Brahmà.———[*To* Mádhavya] Where now, my friend, shall I sit and recreate my sight with the slender shrubs which bear a faint resemblance to the shape of Sacontalá?

Mádh. You will soon see the damsel skilled in painting, whom you informed that you would spend the forenoon in yon bower of Mádhavì creepers: and she will bring the queen's picture which you commanded her to draw.

Dushm. My soul will be delighted even by her picture. ——Show the way to the bower.

Ma'dh. This way, my friend.——[*They both advance,* Misracési *following them.*]—The arbour of twining Mádhavìs, embellished with fragments of stone like bright gems, appears by its pleasantness, though without a voice, to bid thee welcome.—— Let us enter it, and be seated. [*They both sit down in the bower*

Misr. [*Aside.*] From behind these branchy shrubs I shall behold the picture of my Sacontalá.——I will afterwards hasten to report the sincere affection of her husband.

[*She conceals herself.*

Dushm. [*Sighing.*] O my approved friend, the whole adventure of the hermitage is now fresh in my memory.—I informed

J

how deeply I was affected by the first sight of the damsel ; but when she was rejected by me you were not present.—Her name was often repeated by me (how, indeed, should it not ?) in our conversation.—What ! hast thou forgotten, as I had, the whole story ?

Misr. [*Aside.*] The sovereigns of the world must not, I find, be left an instant without the objects of their love.

Mádh. Oh, no : I have not forgotten it ; but at the end of our discourse you assured me that your love tale was invented soley for your diversion ; and this, in the simplicity of my heart, I believed.—Some great event seems in all this affair to be predestined in heaven.

Misr. [*Aside.*] Nothing is more true.

Dushm. [*Having meditated.*] O ! my friend, suggest some relief for my torment.

Mádh. What new pain torments you ? Virtuous men should never be thus afflicted : the most violent wind shakes not mountains.

Dushm. When I reflect on the situation of your friend Sacontalá, who must now be greatly affected by my desertion of her, I am without comfort.—She made an attempt to follow the Bráhmens and the matron : Stay, said the sage's pupil, who was revered as the sage himself ; Stay, said he, with a loud voice. Then once more she fixed on me, who had betrayed her, that celestial face, then bedewed with gushing tears ; and the bare idea of her pain burns me like an envenomed javelin.

Misr. [*Aside.*] How he afflicts himself ! I really sympathize with him.

Mádh. Surely some inhabitant of the heavens must have wafted her to his mansion.

Dushm. No ; what male divinity would have taken the pains to carry off a wife so firmly attached to her lord ? Ménacà, the nymph of Swerga, gave her birth ; and some of her attendant nymphs have, I imagine, concealed her at the desire of her mother.

Misr. [*Aside.*] To reject Sacontalá was, no doubt, the effect of a delirium, not the act of a waking man.

Mádh. If it be thus, you will soon meet her again.

Dushm. Alas! why do you think so?

Mádh. Because no father and mother can long endure to see their daughter deprived of her husband.

Dushm. Was it sleep that impaired my memory? Was it delusion? Was it an error of my judgment? Or was it the destined reward of my bad actions? Whatever it was, I am sensible that, until Sacontalá return to these arms, I shall be plunged in the abyss of affliction.

Mádh. Do not despair: the fatal ring is itself an example that the lost may be found.—Events which were foredoomed by Heaven must not be lamented.

Dushm. [*Looking at his ring.*] The fate of this ring, now fallen from a station which it will not easily regain, I may at least deplore.—O gem, thou art removed from the soft finger, beautiful with ruddy tips on which a place had been assigned thee; and, minute as thou art, thy bad qualities appear from the similiarity of thy punishment to mine.

Misr. [*Aside.*] Had it found a way to any other hand its lot would have been truly deplorable.——O Ménacà, how wouldst thou be delighted with the conversation which gratifies my ears!

Mádh. Let me know, I pray, by what means the ring obtained a place on the finger of Sacontalá.

Dushm. You shall know, my friend.—When I was coming from the holy forest to my capital, my beloved, with tears in her eyes, thus addressed me: "How long will the son of my lord keep me in his remembrance?"

Mádh. Well; what then?

Dushm. Then fixing this ring on her lovely finger, I thus answered: "Repeat each day one of the three syllables engraved on this gem; and before thou hast spelled the word Dushmanta, one of my noblest officers shall attend thee, and conduct my darling to her palace."—Yet I forgot, I deserted her in my phrensy.

Misr. [*Aside.*] A charming interval of three days was fixed between their seperation and their meeting, which the will of Brahmà rendered unhappy.

Mádh. But how came the ring to enter, like a hook, into the mouth of a carp?

Dushm. When my beloved was lifting water to her head in the pool of Sachitirt'ha, the ring must have dropped unseen.

Mádh. It is very probable.

Misr. [*Aside*]. Oh! it was thence that the king, who fears nothing but injustice, doubted the reality of his marriage; but how, I wonder, could his memory be connected with a ring?

Dushm. I am really angry with this gem.

Mádh. [*Laughing.*] So am I with this staff.

Dushm. Why so, Mádhavya?

Mádh. Because it presumes to be so straight when I am so crooked.—Impertinent stick!

Dushm. [*Not attending to him.*] How, O ring, couldst thou leave that hand adorned with soft long fingers, and fall into a pool decked only with water lilies?—The answer is obvious: thou art irrational.—But how could I, who was born with a reasonable soul, desert my only beloved?

Misr. [*Aside.*] He anticipates my remark.

Mádh. [*Aside.*] So; I must wait here during his meditations, and perish with hunger.

Dushm. O my darling, whom I treated with disrespect, and forsook without reason, when will this traitor, whose heart is deeply stung with repentant sorrow, be once more blessed with a sight of thee?

A Damsel *enters with a picture.*

Dáms. Great king, the picture is finished.

[*Holding it before him.*

Dushm. [*Gazing on it.*] Yes; that is her face; those are her beautiful eyes; those her lips embellished with smiles, and surpassing the red lustre of the Carcandhu fruit: her mouth seems, though painted, to speak, and her countenance darts beams of affection blended with a variety of melting tints.

Mádh. Truly, my friend, it is a picture sweet as love itself: my eye glides up and down to feast on every particle of it; and it gives me as much delight as if I were actually conversing with the living Sacontalá.

Misr. [*Aside.*] An exquisite piece of painting!——My beloved friend seems to stand before my eyes.

Dushm. Yet the picture is infinitely below the original; and my warm fancy, by supplying its imperfections, represents, in some degree, the loveliness of my darling.

Misr. [*Aside.*] His ideas are suitable to his excessive love and severe penitence.

Dushm. [*Sighing.*] Alas! I rejected her when she lately approached me, and now I do homage to her picture; like a traveller who negligently passes by a clear and full rivulet, and soon ardently thirsts, for a false appearance of water on the sandy desert.

Mádh. There are so many female figures on this canvas, that I cannot well distinguish the lady Sacontalá.

Misr. [*Aside.*] The old man is ignorant of her transcendent beauty; her eyes, which fascinated the soul of his prince, never sparkled, I suppose, on Mádhavya.

Dushm. Which of the figures do you conceive intended for the queen?

Mádh. [*Examining the picture.*] It is she I imagine, who looks a little fatigue; with the string of her vest rather loose; the slender stalks of her arms falling languidly; a few bright drops on her face, and some flowers dropping from her united locks. That must be the queen; and the rest, I suppose, are her damsels.

Dushm. You judge well; but my affection requires something more in the piece. Besides, through some defect in the coloring, a tear seems trickling down her cheek, which ill suits the state in which I desired to see her painted.—[*To the Damsel.*]—The picture, O Chaturicà, is unfinished.—Go back to the painting room and bring the implements of thy art.

Dams. Kind Mádhavya. hold the picture while I obey the king.

Dushm. No; I will hold it.

[*He takes the picture; and the damsel goes out.*

Mádh. What else is to be painted?

Misr. [*Aside.*] He desires, I presume, to add all those circumstances which became the situation of his beloved in the hermitage.

Dushm. In this landscape, my friend, I wish to see represented the river Málinì, with some amorous Flamingos on its green margin; farther back must appear some hills near the mountain Himálaya, surrounded with herds of Chamaras; and in the foreground, a dark spreading tree, with some mantles of woven bark suspended on its branches to be dried by the sunbeams; while a pair of black antelopes couch in its shade, and the female gently rubs her beautiful forehead on the horn of the male.

Mádh. Add what you please; but, in my judgment, the vacant places should be filled with old hermits, bent, like me, towards the ground.

Dushm. [*Not attending to him.*] Oh! I had forgotten that my beloved herself must have some new ornaments.

Mádh. What I pray?

Misr. [*Aside.*] Such, no doubt, as become a damsel bred in a forest.

Dushm. The artist had omitted a Sirìsha flower with its peduncle fixed behind her soft ear, and its filaments waving over part of her cheek; and between her breasts must be placed a knot of delicate fibres, from the stalks of water lilies, like the rays of an autumnal moon.

Mádh. Why does the queen cover part of her face, as if she was afraid of something, with the tips of her fingers, that glow like the flowers of the Cuvalaya?—Oh! I now perceive an impudent bee, that thief of odours, who seems eager to sip honey from the lotos of her mouth.

Dushm. A bee! drive off the importunate insect.

Mádh. The king has supreme power over all offenders.

Dushm. O male bee, who approachest the lovely inhabitants of a flowery grove, why dost thou expose thyself to the pain of being rejected?—See where thy female sits on a blossom, and, though thirsty, waits for thy return: without thee she will not taste its nectar.

Misr. [*Aside.*] A wild, but apt, address!

Mádh. The perfidy of male bees is proverbial.

Dushm. [*Angrily.*] Shouldst thou touch, O bee, the lip of my darling, ruddy as a fresh leaf on which no wind has yet breathed, a lip from which I drank sweetness in the banquet of love, thou shalt, by my order, be imprisoned in the center of a lotos.—Dost thou still disobey me?

Mádh. How can he fail to obey, since you denounce so severe a punishment?—[*Aside, laughing.*]—He is stark mad with love and affliction; whilst I, by keeping him company, shall be as mad as he without either.

Dushm. After my positive injunction, art thou still unmoved?

Misr. [*Aside.*] How does excess of passion alter even the wife!

Mádh. Why, my friend, it is only a painted bee.

Misr. [*Aside.*] Oh! I perceive his mistake: it shows the perfection of the art. But why does he continue musing?

Dushm. What ill-natured remark was that?—Whilst I am enjoying the rapture of beholding her to whom my soul is attached, thou, cruel remembrancer, tellest me that it is only a picture.—[*Weeping.*]

Misr. [*Aside.*] Such are the woes of a separated lover! He is on all sides, entangled in sorrow.

Dushm. Why do I thus indulge unremitted grief? That intercourse with my darling which dreams would give, is prevented by my continued inability to repose; and my tears will not suffer me to view her distinctly even in this picture.

Misr. [*Aside.*] His misery acquits him entirely of having deserted her in his perfect senses.

The Damsel *re-enters.*

Dams. As I was advancing, O king, with my box of pencils and colors——

Dushm. [*Hastily.*] What happened ?

Dams. It was forcibly seized by the queen Vasumatí, whom her maid Pingalicà had apprised of my errand ; and she said : "I will myself deliver the casket to the son of my lord."

Mádh. How came you to be released ?

Dams. While the queen's maid was disengaging the skirt of her mantle, which had been caught by the branch of a thorny shrub, I stole away.

Dushm. Friend Mádhavya, my great attention to Vasumatì has made her arrogant ; and she will soon be here : be it your care to conceal the picture.

Mádh. [*Aside.*] I wish you would conceal it yourself. ——[*He takes the picture, and rises.*]——[*Aloud.*]—If, indeed, you will disentangle me from the net of your secret apartments, to which I am confined, and suffer me to dwell on the wall Méghach'handa which encircles them, I will hide the picture in a place where none shall see it but pigeons. [*He goes out.*

Misr. [*Aside.*] How honorably he keeps his former engagements, though his heart be now fixed on another object !

A Warder *enters with a leaf.*

Ward. May the king prosper !

Dushm. Warder, hast thou lately seen the queen Vasumatì ?

Ward. I met her, O king ; but when she perceived the leaf in my hand, she retired.

Dushm. The queen distinguishes time : she would not impede my public business.

Ward. The chief minister sends this message : "I have carefully stated a case which has arisen in the city, and accurately committed it to writing : let the king deign to consider it."

Dushm. Give me the leaf.——[*Receiving it, and reading.*] ——"Be it presented at the foot of the king, that a merchant named Dhanavriddhi, who had extensive commerce at sea, was lost in a late ship-wreck: he had no child born; and has left a fortune of many millions, which belong, if the king commands, to the royal treasury."——[*With sorrow.*]—Oh! how great a misfortune it is to die childless! Yet with his affluence he must have had many wives:—let an inquiry be made whether any one of them is pregnant.

Ward. I have heard that his wife, the daughter of an excellent man, named Sácétaca, has already performed the ceremonies usual on pregnancy.

Dushm. The child, though unborn, has a title to his father's property.——Go: bid the minister make my judgment public.

Ward. I obey. [*Going.*

Dushm. Stay a while.——

Ward. [*Returning.*] I am here.

Dushm. Whether he had or had not left offspring, the estate should not have been forfeited.—Let it be proclaimed, that whatever kinsman any one of my subjects may lose, Dushmanta (excepting always the case of forfeiture for crimes) will supply, in tender affection, the place of that kinsman.

Ward. The proclamation shall be made.——[*He goes out.*

[Dushmanta *continues meditating.*]

Re-enter Warder.

O king! the royal decree, which proves that your virtues are awake after a long slumber, was heard with bursts of applause.

Dushm. [*Sighing deeply.*] When an illustrious man dies, alas, without an heir, his estate goes to a stranger; and such will be the fate of all the wealth accumulated by the sons of Puru.

Ward. Heaven avert the calamity! [*Goes out.*

Dushm. Wo is me! I am stripped of all the felicity which I once enjoyed.

Misr. [*Aside.*] How his heart dwells on the idea of his beloved!

Dushm. My lawful wife, whom I basely deserted, remains fixed in my soul: she would have been the glory of my family, and might have produced a son brilliant as the richest fruit of the teeming earth.

Misr. [*Aside.*] She is not forsaken by all; and soon, I trust, will be thine.

Dams. [*Aside.*] What a change has the minister made in the king by sending him that mischievous leaf! Behold, he is deluged with tears.

Dushm. Ah me! the departed souls of my ancestors, who claim a share in the funeral cake, which I have no son to offer, are apprehensive of losing their due honor, when Dushmanta shall be no more on earth:——who then, alas, will perform in our family those obsequies which the Véda prescribes?——My forefathers must drink, instead of a pure libation, this flood of tears, the only offering which a man who dies childless can make them. [*Weeping.*

Misr. [*Aside.*] Such a veil obscures the king's eyes, that he thinks it total darkness, though a lamp be now shining brightly.

Dams. Afflict not yourself immoderately: our lord is young, and when sons illustrious as himself shall be born of other queens, his ancestors will be redeemed from their offences committed here below.

Dushm. [*With agony.*] The race of Puru, which has hitherto been fruitful and unblemished, ends in me; as the river Sereswatì disappears in a region unworthy of her divine stream. [*He faints.*

Dams. Let the king resume confidence.— [*She supports him.*

Misr. [*Aside.*] Shall I restore him? No; he will speedily be roused—I heard the nymph Dévajananî consoling Sacontalá in these words: "As the gods delight in their portion of Sacrifices, thus wilt thou soon be delighted by the love of thy husband." I go, therefore, to raise her spirits, and please my friend Mànacá with an account of his virtues and his affection. [*She rises aloft and disappears.*

Behind the scenes. A Bráhmen must not be slain: save the life of a Bráhmen.

Dushm. [*Reviving and listening.*] Hah ! was not that the plaintive voice of Mádhavya ?

Dams. He has probably been caught with the picture in his hand by Pingalicà and the other maids.

Dushm. Go, Chaturicá, and reprove the queen in my name for not restraining her servants.

Dams. As the king commands. [*She goes out.*

Again behind the scenes. I am a Bráhmen, and must not be put to death.

Dushm. It is manifestly some Bráhmen in great danger.——Hola ! who is there ?

The old Chamberlain *enters.*

Cham. What is the king's pleasure ?

Dushm. Inquire why the faint-hearted Mádhavya cries out so piteously.

Cham. I will know in an instant. [*He goes out, and returns trembling.*

Dushm. Is there any alarm, Párvatáyana ?

Cham. Alarm enough !

Dushm. What causes thy tremor ?—Thus do men tremble through age : fear shakes the old man's body, as the breeze agitates the leaves of the Pippala.

Cham. Oh ! deliver thy friend.

Dushm. Deliver him ! from what ?

Cham. From distress and danger.

Dushm. Speak more plainly.

Cham. The wall which looks to all quarters of the heavens, and is named, from the clouds which cover it, Méghach'handa——

Dushm. What of that ?

Cham. From the summit of that wall, the pinnacle of which is hardly attainable even by the blue-necked pigeons, an evil being, invisible to human eyes, has violently carried away the friend of your childhood.

Dushm. [*Starting up hastily.*] What ! are even my secret

apartments infested by supernatural agents ?—Royalty is ever subjected to molestation.—A king knows not even the mischiefs which his own negligence daily and hourly occasions :—how then should he know what path his people are treading ; and how should he correct their manners when his own are uncorrected ?

Behind the scenes. Oh, help ! Oh, release me.

Dushm. [*Listening and advancing.*] Fear not, my friend, fear nothing——

Behind the scenes. Not fear, when a monster has caught me by the nape of my neck, and means to snap my backbone as he would snap a sugar-cane !

Dushm. [*Darting his eyes round.*] Hola ! my bow——

A Warder *enters with the king's bow and quiver.*

Ward. Here are our great hero's arms.

[Dushmanta *takes his bow and an arrow*

Behind the scenes. Here I stand ; and, thirsting for thy fresh blood, will slay thee struggling as a tiger slays a calf.——Where now is thy protector, Dushmanta, who grasps his bow to defend the oppressed ?

Dushm. [*Wrathfully.*] The demon names me with defiance. —Stay, thou basest of monsters.—Here am I, and thou shalt not long exist.—[*Raising his bow.*]—Show the way, Párvatáyana, to the stairs of the terrace.

Cham. This way, great king !—— [*All go out hastily.*

The SCENE *changes to a broad* TERRACE.

Enter Dushmanta.

Dushm. [*Looking round.*] Ah ! the place is deserted.

Behind the scenes. Save me, oh ! save me—I see thee, my friend, but thou canst not discern me, who, like a mouse in the claws of a cat, have no hope of life.

Dushm. But this arrow shall distinguish thee from thy foe, in spite of the magic which renders thee invisible.——Mádhavya, stand firm ; and thou, blood-thirsty fiend, think not of destroying him whom I love and will protect.—See, I thus fix a shaft which shall pierce thee, who deservest death, and shall save a Bráhmen who deserves long life; as the celestial bird sips the milk, and leaves the water which has been mingled with it. [*He draws the bowstring.*

Enter Mátali *and* Mádhavya.

Mát. The god Indra has destined evil demons to fall by thy shafts; against them let thy bow be drawn, and cast on thy friend's eyes bright with affection.

Dushm. [*Astonished, giving back his arms.*] Oh! Mátali, welcome; I greet the driver of Indra's car.

Mádh. What! this cutthroat was putting me to death, and thou greetest him with a kind welcome!

Mát. [*Smiling.*] O king, live long and conquer! Hear on what errand I am dispatched by the ruler of the firmament.

Dushm. I am humbly attentive.

Mát. There is a race of Dánavas, the children of Cálané-mi, whom it is found hard to subdue—

Dushm. This I have heard already from Náred.

Mát. The god with an hundred sacrifices, unable to quell that gigantic race, commissions thee, his approved friend, to assail them in the front of battle; as the sun with seven steeds despairs of overcoming the dark legions of night, and gives way to the moon, who easily scatters them. Mount, therefore, with me, the car of Indra, and, grasping thy bow, advance to assured victory.

Dushm. Such a mark of distinction from the prince of good geni honors me highly; but say why you treated so roughly my poor friend Mádhavya.

Mát. Perceiving that, for some reason or another, you were grievously afflicted, I was desirous to rouse your spirits by provoking you to wrath.—The fire blazes when wood is thrown on it; the serpent, when provoked, darts his head against the assailant; and a man capable of acquiring glory, exerts himself when his courage is excited.

Dushm. [*To* Mádhavya.] My friend, the command of Divespetir must instantly be obeyed: go, therefore, and carry the intelligence to my chief minister; saying to him in my name: "Let thy wisdom secure my people from danger while this braced bow has a different employment."

Mádh.—I obey; but wish it could have been employed without assistance from my terror. [*He goes out.*

Mát. Ascend, great king.

[Dushmanta *ascends, and* Mátali *drives off the car.*

ACT VII.

Dushmanta *with* Mátali *in the car of* Indra, *supposed to be above the clouds.*

Dushmanta.

I AM sensible, O Mátali, that, for having executed the commission which Indra gave me, I deserved not such a profusion of honors.

Mát. Neither of you is satisfied. You who have conferred so great a benefit on the god of thunder, consider it as a trifling act of devotion; whilst he reckons not all his kindness equal to the benefit conferred.

Dushm. There is no comparison between the service and the reward.—He surpassed my warmest expectation, when, before he dismissed me, he made me sit on half of his throne, thus exalting me before all the inhabitants of the Empyreum; and smiling to see his son Jayanta, who stood near him, ambitious of the same honor, perfumed my bosom with essence of heavenly sandal wood, throwing over my neck a garland of flowers blown in paradise.

Mát. O king, you deserve all imaginable rewards from the sovereign of good genii; whose empyreal feats have twice been disentangled from the thorns of Danu's race; formerly by the claws of the man-lion, and lately by thy unerring shafts.

Dushm. My victory proceeded wholly from the auspices of the god; as on earth, when servants prosper in great enterprises, they owe their success to the magnificence of their lords. ——Could Arun dispel the shades of night if the deity with a thousand beams had not placed him before the car of day?

Mát. That case, indeed, is parallel.—[*Driving slowly.*]—See, O king, the full exaltation of thy glory, which now rides on the back of heaven! The delighted genii have been collecting, among the trees of life, those crimson and azure dyes, with which the celestial damsels tinge their beautiful feet; and they now are writing thy actions in verses worthy of divine melody.

Dushm. [*Modestly.*] In my transport, O Mátali, after the rout of the giants, this wonderful place had escaped my notice.—In what path of the winds are we now journeying?

Mát. This is the way which leads along the triple river, heaven's brightest ornament, and causes yon luminaries to roll in a circle with diffused beams: it is the course of a gentle breeze which supports the floating forms of the gods; and this path was the second step of Vishnu, when he confounded the proud Vali.

Dushm. My internal soul, which acts by exterior organs, is filled by the sight with a charming complacency.——[*Looking at the wheels.*]—We are now passing, I guess, through the region of clouds.

Ma't. Whence do you form that conjecture?

Dushm. The car itself instructs me that we are moving over clouds pregnant with showers; for the circumference of its wheels disperses pellucid water; the horses of Indra sparkle with lightning; and I now see the warbling Chátacas descend from their nests on the summits of mountains.

Ma't. It is even so; and in another moment you will be in the country which you govern.

Dushm. [*Looking down.*] Through the rapid, yet imperceptible, descent of the heavenly steeds, I now perceive the allotted station of men.——Astonishing prospect! It is yet so distant from us, that the low lands appear confounded with the high mountain tops; the trees erect their branchy shoulders, but seem leafless; the rivers look like bright lines, but their waters vanish; and, at this instant, the globe of earth seems thrown upwards by some stupendous power.

Mát. [*Looking with reverence on the earth.*] How delightful is the abode of mankind!—O king, you saw distinctly.

Dushm. Say, Mátali, what mountain is that which, like an evening cloud, pours exhilarating streams, and forms a golden zone between the western and eastern seas?

Mát. That, O king, is the mountain of Gandharvas, named Hémacúta: the universe contains not a more excellent place for the successful devotion of the pious. There Casyapa, father of the immortals, ruler of men, son of Maríchi, who sprang from the self-existent, resides with his comfort Aditi, blessed in holy retirement.

Dushm. [*Devoutly.*] This occasion of attaining good fortune must not be neglected: may I approach the divine pair, and do them complete homage?

Mát. By all means.—It is an excellent idea!—We are now descended on earth.

Dushm. [*With wonder.*] These chariot wheels yield no sound; no dust arises from them; and the descent of the car gave me no shock.

Mát. Such is the difference, O king, between thy car and that of Indra!

Dushm. Where is the holy retreat of Máríchi?

Mát. [*Pointing.*] A little beyond that grove, where you see a pious Yógí, motionless as a pollard, holding his thick bushy hair, and fixing his eyes on the solar orb.—Mark; his body is half covered with a white ant's edifice made of raised clay; the skin of a snake supplies the place of his sacerdotal thread, and part of it girds his loins; a number of knotty plants encircle and wound his neck; and surrounding bird's nests almost conceal his shoulders.

Dushm. I bow to a man of his austere devotion.

Mát. [*Checking the reins.*] Thus far, and enough.—We now enter the sanctuary of him who rules the world, and the groves which are watered by streams from celestial sources.

Dushm. This asylum is more delightful than paradise itself: I could fancy myself bathing in a pool of nectar.

Mát. [*Stopping the car.*] Let the king descend.

Dushm. [*Joyfully descending.*] How canst thou leave the car?

Mát. On such an occasion it will remain fixed: we may both leave it.—This way, victorious hero, this way.—Behold the retreat of the truly pious.

Dushm. I see with equal amazement both the pious and their awful retreat.—It becomes, indeed, pure spirits to feed on balmy air in a forest blooming with trees of life; to bathe in rills dyed yellow with the golden dust of the lotos, and to fortify their virtue in the mysterious bath; to meditate in caves, the pebbles of which are unblemished gems; and to restrain their passions, even though nymphs of exquisite beauty frolic around them: in this grove alone is attained the summit of true piety, to which other hermits in vain aspire.

Mát. In exalted minds the desire of perfect excellence continually increases.—[*Turning aside.*]—Tell me, Vriddhasácalya, in what business is the divine son of Maríchi now engaged?—What sayest thou?—Is he conversing with the daughter of Dacsha, who practises all the virtues of a dutiful wife, and is consulting him on moral questions?—Then we must await his leisure.—[*To* Dushmanta.] Rest, O king, under the shade of this Asóca tree, whilst I announce thy arrival to the father of Indra.

Dushm. As you judge right.——[Mátali *goes out.*—Dushmanta *feels his right arm throb.*] Why, O my arm, dost thou flatter me with a vain omen?—My former happiness is lost, and misery only remains.

Behind the scenes. Be not so restless: in every situation thou showest thy bad temper.

Dushm. [*Listening.*] Hah! this is no place, surely, for a malignant disposition.——Who can be thus rebuked?—[*Looking with surprise.*]—I see a child, but with no childish countenance or strength, whom two female anchorites are endeavouring to keep in order; while he forcibly pulls towards him, in rough play, a lion's whelp with a torn mane, who seems just dragged from the half-sucked nipple of the lioness!

A little Boy *and two female* Attendants *are discovered, as described by the king.*

Boy. Open thy mouth, lion's whelp, that I may count thy teeth.

First Atten. Intractable child! Why dost thou torment

the wild animals of this forest, whom we cherish as if they were our own offspring ?——Thou seemest even to sport in anger. ——Aptly have the hermits named thee Servademana, since thou tamest all creatures.

Dushm. Ah ! what means it that my heart inclines to this boy as if he were my own son ?—[*Meditating.*]—Alas ! I have no son ; and the reflection makes me once more soft-hearted.

Second Atten. The lioness will tear thee to pieces if thou release not her whelp.

Boy. [*Smiling.*] Oh ! I am greatly afraid of her to be sure!

[*He bites his lip, as in defiance of her.*

Dushm. [*Aside, amazed.*] The child exhibits the rudiments of heroic valour, and looks like fire which blazes from the addition of dry fuel.

First Atten. My beloved child, set at liberty this young prince of wild beasts ; and I will give thee a prettier plaything.

Boy. Give it first.—Where is it ? [*Stretching out his hand.*

Dushm. [*Aside, gazing on the child's palm.*] What ! the very palm of his hand bears the marks of empire ; and whilst he thus eagerly extends it, shows its lines of exquisite network, and glows like a lotos expanded at early dawn, when the ruddy splendour of its petals hides all other tints in obscurity.

Second Atten. Mere words, my Suvritá, will not pacify him.—Go, I pray, to my cottage, where thou wilt find a plaything made for the hermit's child, Sancara ; it is a peacock of earthen-ware painted with rich colors.

First Atten. I will bring it speedily. [*She goes out.*

Boy. In the mean time I will play with the young lion.

Second Atten. [*Looking at him with a smile.*] Let him go, I entreat thee.

Dushm. [*Aside.*] I feel the tenderest affection for this unmanageable child. [*Sighing.*]—How sweet must be the delight of virtuous fathers, when they soil their bosoms with dust by lifting up their playful children, who charm them with inarticulate prattle, and show the white blossoms of their teeth, while they laugh innocently at every trifling occurrence !

Second Atten. [*Raising her finger.*] What! dost thou show no attention to me!—[*Looking round.*]—Are any of the hermits near!—[*Seeing* Dushmanta.]—Oh! Let me request you, gentle stranger, to release the lion's whelp, who cannot disengage himself from the grasp of this robust child.

Dushm. I will endeavour.—[*Approaching the* Boy *and smiling.*]—O thou, who art the son of a pious anchorite, how canst thou dishonor thy father, whom thy virtues would make happy, by violating the rules of this consecrated forest? It becomes a black serpent only, to infest the boughs of a fragrant sandal tree. [*The* Boy *releases the lion.*

Second Atten. I thank you, courteous guest;—but he is not the son of an anchorite.

Dushm. His actions, indeed, which are conformable to his robustness, indicate a different birth: but my opinion arose from the sanctity of the place which he inhabits.—[*Taking the* Boy *by the hand.*]—[*Aside.*]—Oh! since it gives me such delight merely to touch the hand of this child, who is the hopeful scion of a family unconnected with mine, what rapture must be felt by the fortunate man from whom he sprang?

Second Atten. [*Gazing on them alternately.*] O wonderful!

Dushm. What has raised your wonder?

Second Atten. The astonishing resemblance between the child and you, gentle stranger, to whom he bears no relation.—It surprised me also to see, that although he has childish humours, and had no former acquaintance with you, yet your words have restored him to his natural good temper.

Dushm. [*Raising the* Boy *to his bosom.*] Holy matron, if he be not the son of a hermit, what then is the name of his family?

Second Atten. He is descended from Puru.

Dushm. [*Aside.*] Hah! thence, no doubt, springs his disposition, and my affection for him.—[*Setting him down.*]—[*Aloud.*] It is, I know, an established usage among the princes of Puru's race, to dwell at first in rich palaces with stuccoed walls, where they protect and cherish the world, but in the decline of life to seek humbler mansions near the roots of venerable trees, where hermits with subdued passions practise austere devotion.—I wonder, however, that this boy, who moves like a god, could have been born of a mere mortal.

Second Atten. Affable stranger, your wonder will cease when you know that his mother is related to a celestial nymph, and brought him forth in the sacred forest of Casyapa.

Dushm. [*Aside.*] I am transported.—This is a fresh ground of hope.—[*Aloud.*]—What virtuous monarch took his excellent mother by the hand?

Second Atten. Oh! I must not give celebrity to the name of a king who deserted his lawful wife.

Dushm. [*Aside.*] Ah! she means me.—Let me now ask the name of the sweet child's mother.—[*Meditating.*]—But it is against good manners to inquire concerning the wife of another man.

The First Attendant *re-enters with a toy.*

First Atten. Look, Servademana, look at the beauty of this bird, Saconta lávanyam.

Boy. [*Looking eagerly round.*] Sacontalá! Oh, where is my beloved mother? [*Both* Attendants *laugh.*

First Atten. He tenderly loves his mother, and was deceived by an equivocal phrase.

Second Atten. My child, she meant only the beautiful shape and colors of this peacock.

Dushm. [*Aside.*] Is my Sacontalá then his mother? Or has that dear name been given to some other woman?—This conversation resembles the fallacious appearance of water in a desert, which ends in bitter disappointment to the stag parched with thirst.

Boy. I shall like the peacock if it can run and fly; not else. [*He takes it.*

First Atten. [*Looking round in confusion.*] Alas, the child's amulet is not on his wrist!

Dushm. Be not alarmed. It was dropped while he was playing with the lion : I see it, and will put it into your hand.

Both. Oh ! beware of touching it.

First Atten. Ah ! he has actually taken it up.

[*They both gaze with surprise on each other.*

Dushm. Here it is ; but why would you have restrained me from touching this bright gem ?

Second Atten. Great monarch, this divine amulet has a wonderful power, and was given to the child by the son of Maríchi, as soon as the sacred rites had been performed after his birth : whenever it fell on the ground, no human being but the father or mother of this boy could have touched it unhurt.

Dushm. What if a stranger had taken it ?

First Atten. It would have become a serpent and wounded him.

Dushm. Have you seen that consequence on any similar occasion ?

Both. Frequently.

Dushm. [*With transport.*] I may then exult on the completion of my ardent desire. [*He embraces the child.*

Second Atten. Come, Suvritá, let us carry the delightful intelligence to Sacontalá, whom the harsh duties of a separated wife have so long oppressed. [*The* Attendants *go out.*

Boy. Farewell ; I must go to my mother.

Dushm. My darling son, thou wilt make her happy by going to her with me.

Boy. Dushmanta is my father ; and you are not Dushmanta.

Dushm. Even thy denial of me gives me delight.

Sacontalá *enters in mourning apparel, with her long hair twisted in a single braid, and flowing down her back.*

Sac. [*Aside.*] Having heard that my child's amulet has proved its divine power, I must either be strangely diffident of my good fortune, or that event which Misracésí predicted has actually happened. [*Advancing.*

Dushm. [*With a mixture of joy and sorrow.*] Ah ! do I see the incomparable Sacontalá clad in sordid weeds ?———Her face is emaciated by the performance of austere duties ; one twisted lock floats over her shoulder ; and with a mind perfectly pure, she supports the long absence of her husband, whose unkindness exceeded all bounds.

Sac. [*Seeing him, yet doubting.*] Is that the son of my lord grown pale with penitence and affliction ?—If not, who is it, that sullies with his touch the hand of my child, whose amulet should have preserved him from such indignity ?

Boy. [*Going hastily to* Sacontalá.] Mother, here is a stranger who calls me son.

Dushm. Oh ! my best beloved, I have treated thee cruelly ; but my cruelty is succeeded by the warmest affection ; and I implore your remembrance and forgiveness.

Sac. [*Aside.*] Be confident, O my heart !—[*Aloud.*]—I shall be most happy when the king's anger has passed away.—

Sac. [*Aside.*]—This must be the son of my lord.

Dushm. By the kindness of heaven, O loveliest of thy sex, thou standest again before me, whose memory was obscured by the gloom of fassination ; as the star Róhinì at the end of an eclipse rejoins her beloved moon.

Sac. May the king be— [*She bursts into tears.*

Dushm. My darling, though the word victorious be suppressed by thy weeping, yet I must have victory, since I see thee again, though with pale lips and a body unadorned.

Boy. What man is this, mother ?

Sac. Sweet child, ask the divinity, who presides over the fortunes of us both. [*She weeps.*

Dushm. O my only beloved, banish from thy mind my cruel desertion of thee.—A violent phrensy overpowered my soul.—Such, when the darkness of illusion prevails, are the actions of the best intentioned ; as a blind man, when a friend binds his head with a wreath of flowers, mistakes it for a twining snake, and foolishly rejects it. [*He falls at her feet.*

Sac. Rise, my husband, oh ! rise—My happiness has been

long interrupted; but joy now succeeds to affliction, since the son of my lord still loves me.—[*He rises.*]—How was the remembrance of this unfortunate woman restored to the mind of my lord's son ?

Dushm. When the dart of misery shall be wholly extracted from my bosom, I will tell you all ; but since the anguish of my soul has in part ceased, let me first wipe off that tear which trickles from thy delicate eye-lash ; and thus efface the memory of all the tears which my delirium has made thee shed.

[*He stretches out his hand.*

Sac. [*Wiping off her tears, and seeing the ring on his finger.*] Ah ! is that the fatal ring !

Dushm. Yes ; by the surprising recovery of it my memory was restored.

Sac. Its influence, indeed, has been great ; since it has brought back the lost confidence of my husband.

Dushm. Take it then, as a beautiful plant receives a flower from the returning season of joy.

Sac. I cannot again trust it.—Let it be worn by the son of my lord.

Mátali *enters.*

Mát. By the will of heaven the king has happily met his beloved wife, and seen the countenance of his little son.

Dushm. It was by the company of my friend that my desire attained maturity.—But say, was not this fortunate event previously known to Indra ?

Mát. [*Smiling.*] What is unknown to the gods ?—But come: the divine Marícha desires to see thee.

Dushm. Beloved, take our son by the hand ; and let me present you both to the father of immortals.

Sac. I really am ashamed, even in thy presence, to approach the deities.

Dushm. It is highly proper on so happy an occasion—Come, I intreat thee. [*They all advance.*

The scene is withdrawn, and Casyapa *is discovered on a throne conversing with* Aditi.

Cas. [*Pointing to the king.*] That, O daughter of Dacsha, is the hero who led the squadrons of thy son to the front of battle, a sovereign of the earth, Dushmanta ; by the means of whose bow the thunder-bolt of Indra (all its work being accomplished) is now a mere ornament of his heavenly palace.

Adi. He bears in his form all the marks of exalted majesty.

Mát. [*To* Dushmanta.] The parents of the twelve Adityas, O king, are gazing on thee, as on their own offspring, with eyes of affection.—Approach them, illustrious prince.

Dushm. Are those, O Mátali, the divine pair, sprung from Marichi and Dacsha ?—Are those the grand-children of Brahmá to whom the self-existent gave birth in the beginning ; whom inspired mortals pronounce the fountain of glory apparent in the form of twelve suns ; they who produced my benefactor, the lord of a hundred sacrifices, and ruler of three worlds ?

Mát, Even they—[*Prostrating himself with* Dushmanta.]—Great beings, the king Dushmanta, who has executed the commands of your son Vasava, falls humbly before your throne.

Cas. Continue long to rule the world.

Adi. Long be a warrior with a car unshattered in combat.

[Sacontalá *and her son prostrate themselves.*

Cas. Daughter, may thy husband be like Indra ! May thy son resemble Jayanta ! And mayst thou (whom no benediction could better suit) be equal in prosperity to the daughter of Pulóman !

Adi. Preserve, my child, a constant unity with thy lord : and may this boy, for a great length of years, be the ornament and joy of you both ! Now be seated near us. [*They all sit down.*

Cas. [*Looking at them by turns.*] Sacontalá is the model of excellent wives ; her son is dutiful ; and thou, O king, hast three rare advantages, true piety, abundant wealth, and active virtue.

Dushm. O divine being, having obtained the former object of my most ardent wishes, I now have reached the summit of earthly happiness through thy favor, and thy benizon will ensure its permanence.—First appears the flower, then the fruit; first clouds are collected, then the shower falls: such is the regular course of causes and effects; and thus, when thy indulgence preceded, felicity generally followed.

Mát. Great indeed, O king, has been the kindness of the primeval Bráhmens.

Dushm. Bright son of Maríchi, this thy handmaid was married to me by the ceremony of Gandharvas, and, after a time, was conducted to my palace by some of her family; but my memory having failed through delirium, I rejected her, and thus committed a grievous offence against the venerable Canna, who is of thy divine lineage: afterwards, on seeing this fatal ring, I remembered my love and my nuptials; but the whole transaction yet fills me with wonder. My soul was confounded with strange ignorance that obscured my senses; as if a man were to see an elephant marching before him, yet to doubt what animal it could be, till he discovered by the traces of his large feet that it was an elephant.

Cas. Cease, my son, to charge thyself with an offence committed ignorantly, and, therefore, innocently.—Now hear me—

Dushm. I am devoutly attentive:

Cas. When the nymph Ménacá led Sacontalá from the place where thy desertion of her had afflicted her soul, she brought her to the palace of Aditi; and I knew, by the power of meditation on the Supreme Being, that thy forgetfulness of thy pious and lawful consort had proceeded from the imprecation of Durvasas, and that the charm would terminate on the sight of thy ring.

Dushm. [*Aside*] My name then is cleared from infamy.

Sac. Happy am I that the son of my lord, who now recognises me, denied me through ignorance, and not with real aversion.——The terrible imprecation was heard, I suppose, when my mind was intent on a different object, by my two beloved friends, who, with extreme affection, concealed it from me to spare my feelings, but advised me at parting to show the ring if my husband should have forgotten me.

Cas. [*Turning to* Sacontalá.] Thou art apprised, my daughter, of the whole truth, and must no longer resent the behaviour of thy lord.——He rejected thee when his memory was impaired by the force of a charm ; and when the gloom was dispelled, his conjugal affection revived ; as a mirror whose surface has been sullied, reflects no image ; but exhibits perfect resemblances when its polish has been restored.

Dushm. Such, indeed, was my situation.

Cas. My son Dushmanta, hast thou embraced thy child by Sacontalá, on whose birth I myself performed the ceremonies prescribed in the Véda ?

Dushm. Holy Maríchi, he is the glory of my house.

Cas. Know too, that his heroic virtue will raise him to a dominion extended from sea to sea : before he has passed the ocean of mortal life, he shall rule, unequalled in combat, this earth with seven peninsulas ; and, as he now is called Servademana, because he tames even in childhood the fiercest animals, so, in his riper years, he shall acquire the name of Bhereta, because he shall sustain and nourish the world.

Dushm. A boy educated by the son of Maríchi, must attain the summit of greatness.

Adi. Now let Sacontalá, who is restored to happiness, convey intelligence to Canna of all these events : her mother Ménacá is in my family, and knows all that has passed.

Sac. The goddess proposes what I most ardently wish.

Cas. By the force of true piety the whole scene will be present to the mind of Canna.

Dushm. The devout sage must be still excessively indignant at my frantic behaviour.

Cas. [*Meditating.*] Then let him hear from me the delightful news, that his foster-child has been tenderly received by her husband, and that both are happy with the little warrior who sprang from them.—Hola ! who is in waiting ?

A Pupil *enters.*

Pup. Great being, I am here.

Cas. Hasten, Golava, through the light air, and in my name inform the venerable Canna, that Sacontalá has a charming son by Dushmanta, whose affection for her was restored with his remembrance, on the termination of the spell raised by the angry Durvásas.

Pup. As the divinity commands. [*He goes out.*

Cas. My son, reascend the car of Indra with thy consort and child, and return happy to thy imperial seat.

Dushm. Be it as Maríchi ordains.

Cas. Henceforth may the god of the atmosphere with copious rain give abundance to thy affectionate subjects; and mayst thou with frequent sacrifices maintain the thunderer's friendship! By numberless interchanges of good offices between you both, may benefits reciprocally be conferred on the inhabitants of the two worlds!

Dushm. Powerful being, I will be studious, as far as I am able to attain that felicity.

Cas. What other favors can I bestow on thee?

Dushm. Can any favors exceed those already bestowed?—— Let every king appply himself to the attainment of happiness for his people; let Sereswatí, the goddess of liberal arts, be adored by all readers of the Véda; and may Siva, with an azure neck and red locks, eternally potent and self-existing, avert from me the pain of another birth in this perishable world, the seat of crimes and of punishment. [*All go out.*

FINIS.

Printed at the Britannia Press, No. 1, Wellington Street, Calcutta.